GOD'S COVENANTS AND RESTORATIONS

by

Victor Vadney

Desert Willow Publishing

God's Covenants and Restorations

By Victor Vadney

Desert Willow Publishing, P O Box 7719, Abilene, TX 79608

Printed by Lightning Source Inc.

ISBN 978-0-9830327-2-4

Photography by Janet Vadney

Contents

Chapter 1: Foundational Concepts & Early Covenants 9
Introduction to Biblical Covenants 9
General Overview of Our Covenant-Making God................................11
God's Covenant with Adam 12
Restoration of God's Covenant with Adam 14
God's Covenant with Noah 16
Part I: Prior to and Including the Flood 16
Part II: After the Flood 16
Restoration of God's Covenant with Noah 17
God's Covenant with Abraham 18
Restorations of God's Covenant with Abraham.................................. 20
Study Questions 26

Chapter 2: Mosaic Covenant: Moses to Solomon 27
Moses as a Restorer 29
Joshua as a Restorer 30
The Judges as Restorers 31
King David as a Restorer 34
King Solomon as a Restorer 36
Study Questions 39

Chapter 3: Mosaic Covenant: Asa to the Prophets 41
King Asa as a Restorer 41
King Jehoshaphat as a Restorer 42
King Joash & Priest Jehoiada as Restorers 44
King Amaziah as a Restorer 45
King Azariah (Uzziah) as a Restorer 47
King Jotham as a Restorer 48
King Hezekiah as a Restorer 48
King Manasseh as a Restorer 49
King Josiah as a Restorer 51
The Prophets as Restorers 53
Study Questions 55

Chapter 4: Mosaic Covenant: Daniel to the Maccabees..................57
Daniel and His Friends as Restorers..57
Jeshua & Zerubbabel as Restorers..59
Ezra as a Restorer..62
Nehemiah as a Restorer 63
Cyrus and Artaxerxes as Restorers 64
The Maccabees as Restorers..66
Study Questions 69

Chapter 5: God's Covenant with David... 71
Restorations of God's Covenant with David 73
God's Preservation of the Earthly House of David.............................. 73
God's Revival of the House of David in Christ 74
Study Questions 76

Chapter 6: God's New Covenant with Jesus Christ 77
Restorations of God's Covenant with Jesus Christ............................... 80
Apostles & Prophets as Restorers of the New Covenant...................... 81
Study Questions 85

Chapter 7: The New Covenant—The Gospels 87
The Gospels as the Cornerstone of Restored Faith............................... 87
Christ Bears Witness about Himself..88
John the Baptist Bears Witness about Christ 89
Christ's Miracles Bear Witness about Christ 89
The Father Bears Witness about Christ..93
The Scriptures Bear Witness about Christ 93
Moses Bears Witness about Christ...97
Study Questions 98

Chapter 8: New Covenant—Acts...99
Acts as a Restoration Pattern for Conversion 99
Acts as a Restoration Pattern for The Church..................................... 105
Establishment & the Nature of the NT Church................................... 106
Acts as a Restoration Pattern of Church Leadership...........................113
Restoration Pattern for Church Autonomy 116
Study Questions 118

Chapter 9: New Covenant—Romans to Ephesians 121
The Pauline Epistles as Restoration Documents................................ 121
Romans 122
1 Corinthians.. 123
2 Corinthians.. 125
Galatians 126
Ephesians 132
Study Questions 134

Chapter 10: New Covenant—Philippians to 2 Thessalonians 135
The Pauline Epistles as Restoration Documents................................ 135
Philippians.. 135
Colossians 138
1 Thessalonians... 140
2 Thessalonians... 142
Study Questions 146

Chapter 11: New Covenant—1 Timothy to Philemon 147
The Pauline Epistles as Restoration Documents................................ 147
1 Timothy.. 147
2 Timothy.. 152
Titus 155
Philemon 157
Study Questions..158

Chapter 12: New Covenant—Paul's Points.................................. 161
Prominent Points in the Pauline Epistles 161
Regarding God and Christ 161
Regarding the Church 162
Regarding God's Righteous, Salvation, & Justification..................... 163
God Grants a Responsive Faith.. 163
Regarding Life in the Spirit 164
Regarding Jews and Gentiles... 164
Regarding the Mosaic Law 165
Regarding Support for Preachers.. 165
Regarding the Christian Life.. 166
Regarding Preachers 166

Regarding What Should be Taught 166
Regarding Inspiration........ 169
Regarding Paul's Apostleship 169
Study Questions 169

Chapter 13: God's Covenant of Marriage 171
God's View of Marriage........ 171
Christ's Teaching on Marriage........ 175
Is There A Pauline Privilege in 1 Corinthians 7? 177
Summary of Paul's Points in 1 Corinthians 7 183
Conclusion 184
Study Questions 185

Conclusions 187
Regarding God's Covenants and Restorations........ 187
Covenant with Adam........ 187
Covenant with Noah & Abraham........ 187
Covenant with Moses........ 188
Covenant with Jesus........ 189
Covenant of Marriage 191
What Should be Restored?........ 191

Bibliography 195

Dedication &Acknowledgements

First I want to thank God for answering my prayers regarding this project. I was convicted that we needed material regarding restoration for the edification of our Ghanaian brethren among whom I have ministered for twelve years, but I did not know even how to begin. I'm thankful that God answers our prayers and He helps us understand His Word and His Will (Colossians 1:3-12). To Him and for Him this book is dedicated.

Second, I want to express sincere thanks to David T. Lusk for his book entitled *God of the Covenant: A Study of Biblical Covenants*, © 1994. In his book, Brother Lusk discusses in depth the Biblical Covenants. Truly, Brother Lusk opened my mind to the concept of God's covenants in the Bible, and for that I am very grateful. I called him on 19 April 2011, and he gave me permission to quote his work. Thank you very much, David Lusk, for your kindness.

Third, I want to thank my wife, Janet, who has spent countless hours proofreading, editing, and helping with the cover. She has been a continual partner in the ministry in Ghana, and has also written material for the edification and instruction of our Ghanaian sisters in Christ.

Fourth, I want to thank the many people who have read this book and have given me constructive criticism, correction, and encouragement. Foremost of those are Elder Travis Smith, Elder Jim Wilson, Sister Bennie Mouser, and Sister Nelda Roberson. Thank you all.

Introduction

This book emphasizes that our God is a covenant-making God. There are three major observations regarding this:

1. God always communicates with man within the framework of covenants.
2. Within a covenant, God often brings about covenant restoration.
3. There are serious consequences to breaking covenant with God.

This book delineates various covenants of the Bible. However, we will not study the many covenants between men in the Bible. Rather, we will study the major covenants God made with man in the Old and New Testaments. We do this so we can understand fully how God has graciously obligated Himself to us, and therefore, what He expects of us in this covenant relationship with Him.

As we study these covenants we will also consider God's restorations of these covenants. These restorations of God's covenants emphasize how committed God is to His covenant relationships with man. We must learn an important lesson here, that is, we too must be committed to restoration of the New Covenant.

The material in this book is organized into 13 chapters for the convenient use in a quarterly Sunday School program.

Chapter 1

Foundational Concepts & Early Covenants

Introduction to Biblical Covenants

The vast majority of references classify Biblical Covenants as being either legal agreements between people, or covenants between God and people (that is, a "theological covenant"). Although these simplified descriptions are informative, they lack descriptive clarity. According to Lusk, the major characteristics of covenants found in the Bible are as follows:

1. **Unilateral Covenant**: In this type of covenant, one party obligates himself, but the other does not, yet still receives the blessings. A good example of this is God's covenant with Noah symbolized by the rainbow.
2. **Parity Treaty**: In this type of covenant, there is a mutual contract that is accepted by both parties. Good examples of this are the covenants between Jacob and Laban (Genesis 31:44-54), and between David and Jonathan (1 Samuel 20:8; 23:18). God doesn't make this kind of covenant with men because God and men are not equals.
3. **Suzerainty Treaty**: In this type of covenant, there is a one-sided regulation imposed by a superior party on an inferior party.

> The inferior party cannot change the terms of the covenant, but can elect to be in the covenant or out of the covenant. In making this covenant, there is a bond in blood. This is illustrated when God issues a life and death bond, a covenant in blood, such as God's covenant Abraham (Genesis 15:5-21) or with Israel (Jeremiah 34:18-19) (Lusk, 1994, pp. 18-19).

In addition, according to Lusk, ancient covenants generally manifested at least some of the following pattern:

1. Preamble. God introduces Himself.
2. Historical Prologue. God's kind deeds are recounted.
3. Invitation to enter the Covenant. (As example see Exodus 19:5).
4. Terms of the Covenant. What man must do to keep the covenant.
5. Blessings and Curses. Consequences of keeping and breaking the covenant.
6. Oath-Swearing Ceremony. In this ceremony, a bloody sacrifice is invoked where the inferior party identifies with the life and blood of the substitute. It implies that this penalty must be paid for breaking the oath.
7. Ceremonies after Ratification. These include feasts, gifts, changing of name, monuments, and memorials.
8. Storage of the Covenant.
9. Witnesses of the Covenant. This would include "heaven and earth" in many covenants that God made with man.
10. Covenant Renewal. These include sacrifices such as offering a lamb.
11. Sign of the Covenant. An example is circumcision in God's Covenant with Abraham (Lusk, 1994, pp. 20-26).

As we explore the covenants initiated by God, we will see at least some parts of this pattern used repeatedly.

General Overview of Our Covenant-Making God

From the beginning of time God has always communicated with man within the framework of a covenant. There were no approved relationships with God outside of a God-initiated covenant with man. Man cannot initiate a covenant with God. It is God who makes covenants with men.

God established a covenant with the whole family of man through **Adam**. Did God have a covenant relationship with all people prior to Christ? Yes, through Adam came the understanding that all peoples must obey God.

God established another covenant with the whole family of man through **Noah**. Through Noah came the understanding that all nations must respect life and institute a system of justice. Through Noah also came the understanding that God hates evil and will most certainly judge it severely. Indeed, it was this covenant with Noah which showed that every country was under God's sovereignty. This is the very reason why God could send Jonah to the Assyrians in Nineveh with a message of judgment. This is also the reason God could judge and overthrow the Gentile nations when they would not repent (see Amos chapter 1; Isaiah chapters 10 & 13 to 24; Jeremiah chapters 46 to 51).

God established another covenant with **Abraham** and his offspring through Isaac and Jacob. Through this family, God would bring forth the Messiah, making Him a blessing for all nations. Through Abraham's offspring the Jewish nation was born according to God's promise. Through Abraham, God made it clear how important faith and obedience are in His eyes.

God established a limited covenant with the Jewish people through **Moses**. That covenant ceased to have authority when the New Covenant was established. This covenant was given for the purpose of bringing the Jews to Christ (Galatians 3:24-25).

God also established a covenant with **David**, that his throne would be eternal. This was fulfilled in Jesus Christ.

God made available the **New Covenant** to the whole family of man through Jesus Christ, the Son of God. It is this covenant under which we live today.

Lastly, God established the **Marriage Covenant** between Himself and the husband and wife.

We will now explore in more detail each of these covenants.

God's Covenant with Adam

Genesis chapters one and two describe the beginning of creation. God's crowning act was the creation of man in God's own image (Genesis 1:26-27). He gave to man dominion over all creation. God was very pleased with the creation, and on the seventh day God rested from all the work He had done in creation (Genesis 2:3). This account shows that God is both the Creator and Ruler of all creation.

God made a special place for Adam called the Garden in Eden. There God made every good plant and tree for food. He placed the tree of life in the midst of the garden. He also created the tree of the knowledge of good and evil. God took the man and put him in the Garden of Eden to work it and keep it. There God gave him the following command:

> [15] Then the LORD God took the man and put him into the garden
> of Eden to cultivate it and keep it. [16] The LORD God commanded
> the man, saying, "From any tree of the garden you may eat freely;
> [17] but from the tree of the knowledge of good and evil you shall
> not eat, for in the day that you eat from it you shall surely die."
> Genesis 2:15-17 (NASB)

Thus, Adam was given great freedom in what he could eat. Adam was not given any commandment carrying any serious consequence except for one, and that was he could not eat from the tree of the knowledge of good and evil. We should note that at this point of time, Adam had not sinned. He did not have personal knowledge of sin or death. However, since God gave Adam the command, it is reasonable to assume that Adam could, in fact, both believe God and obey God.

From this very beginning of interaction between God and His creature man, God desired to bless man and to have fellowship with him. However, God highly valued obedience amongst His creatures. God has the right to have such values, because He was both the Creator and Ruler of all creation. It is clear from Scripture that God already had a similar relationship of belief and obedience with His angels in Heaven:

> [6] And angels who did not keep their own domain, but abandoned their proper abode, He has kept in eternal bonds under darkness for the judgment of the great day. Jude 1:6 (NASB)

> [4] For if God did not spare angels when they sinned, but cast them into hell and committed them to pits of darkness, reserved for judgment.... 2 Peter 2:4 (NASB)

Therefore, the tree of the knowledge of good and evil became a symbolic test of faith in God and obedience to God. It took one who had already violated both faith and obedience to God to exploit this situation and bring about the fall of man. That creature was Satan. Satan convinced Eve that God had lied about the consequences of eating the fruit of the tree of the knowledge of good and evil. He enticed her to eat of this fruit, and Eve then shared it with her husband. God then pronounced judgment on the serpent (Satan), Eve, and Adam. Satan was cursed. The humans were driven out of the Garden of Eden because they had lost that close fellowship with God. Spiritually they died that very day, and physically they would also die. Satan said that they would not die if they ate the forbidden fruit. However, the genealogy of Genesis chapter 5 repeats the same phrase after each and every person, saying, "...and he died." Therefore, Satan is a liar and the father of lies (John 8:44), for he contradicted God, saying Adam and Eve would NOT die. Adam and Eve believed Satan instead of God and their actions followed their beliefs. Therefore, they bore the penalty that God had spoken of beforehand, the same penalty that they had rejected as false because of Satan's deception.

There are some who object, saying that the word "covenant" is not in the creation account and that we must not use this word here. Although we do not find the word "covenant" prior to Genesis 6:18, we can still be certain that God made a covenant with Adam from the book of Hosea—

> [7] But like Adam they have transgressed the covenant;
> There they have dealt treacherously against Me. Hosea 6:7 (NASB)

The form of this covenant is a Suzerainty Treaty in type. Here we have God who is infinitely greater making a covenant with His own creation, even man. It can be outlined as follows:

1. Two Parties – God and Adam—Adam was the representative of the human race.
2. Conditions imposed on Adam—obedience was demanded. Adam was commanded not to eat of the tree of the knowledge of good and evil.
3. Implied Promises of God—eternal life, represented by the tree of life.
4. Threat of Death for Disobedience. (Lusk, 1994, pp. 35-36)

This account shows that from the very beginning God had no fellowship with man except through covenants. We will find this repeatedly as we look at other covenants initiated by God. God's covenant with Adam also shows that God definitely has expectations of man when God comes into a covenant relationship with man. That expectation is that man must believe and obey God, who is his Creator and Ruler.

Restoration of God's Covenant with Adam

In one sense, there can be no restoration of this covenant because there is now neither a Garden of Eden nor a tree of the knowledge of good and evil. However, the consequences of this covenant have been active for every son and daughter of Adam ever since that terrible day when our ancient parents chose to believe and follow Satan rather than God. One consequence is death, and it rules over us and brings every son and daughter of Adam and Eve into its dominion. Only in Christ can we escape from this awful conclusion:

> [20] But now Christ has been raised from the dead, the first fruits of those who are asleep. [21] For since by a man came death, by a man also came the resurrection of the dead. [22] For as in Adam all die, so also in Christ all shall be made alive. 1 Corinthians 15:20-22 (NASB)

Aside from death, this has other consequences for man today. Every man and woman on this planet will do something wrong and feel guilty about it, for we knew it was wrong and we did it anyway. We all come to understand the knowledge of good and evil, and we are all guilty before God for doing evil. The knowledge of good and evil has deeply impressed our consciences, and surely we are defiled by it. It is not that we have "inherited" Adam's sin as some teach. Rather, just as Adam was not condemned for Eve's sin but his own, so each of us is condemned because we all sin:

> 12 Therefore, just as through one man sin entered into the world, and death through sin, and so death spread to all men, because all sinned. Romans 5:12 (NASB)

Just as God's covenant with Adam demanded faith and obedience, so God still has these most basic expectations of faith and obedience for us even to this day. Adam sinned not just because he ate the forbidden fruit, but because Eve convinced him that God was wrong and Satan was right (Genesis 3:17). Sin always has its roots in a lack of faith in God and what God has said. Some say this is a covenant of works, but it is more than that, for it mandates believing God above anyone else. When we lack that faith, we too will fail in our obligations toward God. Because of this lack of faith, we will not be able to justify ourselves before Him.

Therefore, God's covenant with Adam introduces the vital need for man's justification before God apart from law, and this can only be fulfilled in Christ. If one is without Christ, then he is lost because he has no access to the cleansing blood of Christ and therefore cannot stand before God justified. No man can stand before God and be justified based on his own works. We need a Savior, One who can justify us by faith, and God gave us the promise of that Savior in Genesis 3:15. As Scripture says,

> 15 "And I will put enmity
> Between you and the woman,
> And between your seed and her seed;
> He shall bruise you on the head,
> And you shall bruise him on the heel." Genesis 3:15 (NASB) (see also Hebrews 2:14-15)

Yes, the consequences of the covenant God made with Adam still reign supreme over man because every one of us will die. However, we have eternal hope and deliverance in Christ.

God's Covenant with Noah

God calls this a covenant in Genesis 6:18. In actuality, God's covenant with Noah is in two parts. The first part is prior to the flood, and the second part is after the flood.

Part I: Prior to and Including the Flood (Genesis 6:9-8:19)

1. The Parties Involved: God and Noah, and through Noah was included his family and the human race. In addition, it included all animal life.
2. Conditions of Obedience: Build the ark and gather the animals and provisions into the ark. This was an enormous undertaking that spanned many decades. Noah was completely obedient to God's commands.
3. Promise: God promised that Noah and his family and the animals with him would be saved from the massive flood.

No threat was openly stated. However, no threat was needed because Noah was faithful to all of God's Commandments. Clearly if Noah had refused to obey God's command to build the Ark, he too would have been destroyed by the flood. Therefore, this portion of the covenant God made with Noah carried with it an implied threat.

Part II: After the Flood (Genesis 8:20-10:32)

1. The Parties: God, Noah and his family, and all animals.
2. Conditions of Obedience: God commanded the family of man through Noah not to eat blood and that they must institute capital punishment for murder.
3. God made the following promises: "while the Earth remains"

(Genesis 8:22), God would not curse the ground again because of man (Genesis 8:21), God would not strike down all the creatures again (Genesis 8:21), God would never again use a flood to cut off all flesh, and God would never use the flood again to destroy the earth (Genesis 9:11).

4. The Sign of Covenant: The rainbow (Genesis 9:13-17). The rainbow serves to continuously reassure man that God will not destroy the earth by a massive flood again.

Many people would affirm that God's Covenant with Noah was a Unilateral Covenant where God bound Himself without any obligation from man. However, Noah was required to do an enormous amount of work for many years in building the ark before the flood. This work included not only building the ark, but also preaching to that lost generation in hope that some might repent (2 Peter 2:5). In addition, the clear command of God after the flood based on the preciousness of life meant that Noah and the family of man must not eat blood. They also were required to administer capital punishment for murder. Therefore, it does not appear that the entirety of God's covenant with Noah was a Unilateral Covenant because God certainly laid substantial requirements on Noah and his offspring.

It is true that God bound Himself to not destroy the earth again with water, and that portion of God's covenant with Noah and the family of man is unilateral and without expectations on the part of man. It should be noted that God responded with this promise after Noah freely offered sacrifices after coming out of the Ark. However, in view of the enormous work required of Noah and in view of the post-Flood commandments, it would seem to be an oversimplification to call the whole of God's Covenant with Noah a Unilateral Covenant that carried no obligations for Noah and the family of man. I would prefer to call the majority of this covenant a Suzerainty Treaty because of God's commands.

Restoration of God's Covenant with Noah

We have God's word that he will not destroy the world with a massive flood again. The rainbow is a sign and symbol of that covenant and

God restores and renews that covenant every time He puts a rainbow in the sky.

Moreover, God's salvation of Noah and his family from Satan's domain by means of water is symbolic of the salvation from sin that we obtain in the waters of baptism. Peter makes this clear in the following passage:

> [18] For Christ also died for sins once for all, the just for the unjust, in order that He might bring us to God, having been put to death in the flesh, but made alive in the spirit; [19] in which also He went and made proclamation to the spirits now in prison, [20] who once were disobedient, when the patience of God kept waiting <u>in the days of Noah, during the construction of the ark, in which a few, that is, eight persons, were brought safely through the water</u>. [21] And corresponding to that, <u>baptism now saves you</u>—not the removal of dirt from the flesh, but an appeal to God for a good conscience—through the resurrection of Jesus Christ, [22] who is at the right hand of God, having gone into heaven, after angels and authorities and powers had been subjected to Him. 1 Peter 3:18-22 (NASB)

God's Covenant with Abraham

Jewish history started with Abraham. God's covenant with Abraham is a very important covenant for both Jews and Christians. Many people say that this was a Unilateral Covenant, that is, God unilaterally bound himself to Abraham without making any demands on Abraham. However, God placed demands on Abraham.

First, ***faith*** was essential to the relationship Abraham had with God. Paul taught repeatedly that justification was by faith and not by works of Mosaic Law, and used Abraham as the prime example of this (see Genesis 15:6; Romans 4:1-25; Galatians 3:6-9, 18). Therefore, God required that Abraham have faith (Hebrews 11:6).

Second, James used Abraham as one who was "...justified by ***works*** when he offered up Isaac his son on the altar..." (James 2:21-24). James contends that "...faith without works is dead..." (James 2:26). James made it clear that Christians must have a working faith.

Over 1400 years later Martin Luther became very upset over the supposed difference between Paul and James, so much so that he called the epistle of James an epistle of straw, and insisted that man was saved by faith ONLY. However, we must not, like Luther, pit the New Testament against itself and say that there is a contradiction. Rather, we must understand that Biblical faith always works. The writer of Hebrews says, "By faith Abraham, when he was tested, offered up Isaac…" (Hebrews 11:17). The writer of Hebrews repeatedly uses this phrase, "By faith," to show that obedience always follows faith (Hebrews 11:3-11, 17, 20-33). Paul summed up this principle that works always follows faith in the following passage:

> [8] For by grace you have been saved through faith; and that not of yourselves, it is the gift of God; [9] not as a result of works, so that no one may boast. [10] For we are His workmanship, created in Christ Jesus for good works, which God prepared beforehand so that we would walk in them. Ephesians 2:8-10 (NASB)

Therefore, there is no a contradiction between Paul and James. Neither Paul nor James believed we can be saved by meritorious works of the Mosaic Law. Faith always works, just like Abraham also did good works after God reckoned righteousness to Abraham because of his faith (Genesis 15:5-6). James insisted that faith without works is dead (James 2:26), and this is consistent with Paul's statement in Ephesians 2:10.

In the following, the outline of God's covenant with Abraham follows that of Lusk, but I have inserted the "blessings" and the "obedience required" sections which appear to be part of the covenant.

1. Preamble/Historical Prologue (Genesis 15:1; 17:1)
2. Invitation (Genesis 12:1-5)
3. Blessings—God promised Abraham that he would become a great nation, that all the families of earth would be blessed in him (Genesis 12:2-3), that he would have a son and that his descendents would be numerous (Genesis 15:4-6), that Abraham would be the father of a multitude of nations, that Canaan would be their homeland (Genesis 17:1-8).
4. Ratification (Genesis 15:1-20)

5. Obedience that was required: travel hundreds of miles to a land he had never known to become a wandering shepherd without any land to call his own (Genesis 12:1-9); the covenant of circumcision (Genesis 17:1-14); the sacrifice of Isaac (Genesis 22:1-18); and all the commands of God (Genesis 26:5).
6. Sign of the Covenant—circumcision (Genesis 17:10-14; Acts 7:8)
7. Oath swearing (Genesis 22:16-18)
8. Changing of the name Abram to Abraham (Genesis 17:5) (Lusk, 1994, pp. 43-46)

Therefore, the covenant God made with Abraham developed over about 25 years. Acts of obedience were required from the beginning with God's command for Abraham to leave his country and trust in God, and these acts of obedience continued many years after God ratified the covenant. However, it should be apparent that without those acts of obedience on Abraham's part, God's covenant with Abraham could not have been sustained. Therefore, it does not seem wise to assert that this was a unilateral covenant because there were clear-cut obligations that Abraham had to demonstrate. Thus, God's covenant with Abraham appears to resemble more a Suzerainty Treaty because of these undeniable conditions, the violations of which would have damaged, if not totally destroyed the covenant relationship.

Restorations of God's Covenant with Abraham

God as the Restorer

It is interesting that God Himself renewed and restored His covenant with Abraham. As mentioned above, the covenant with Abraham evolved over a period of about 25 years. Through this time God was working with Abraham so that Abraham could display in his life persistent faith and faithfulness to God. For example, when Abraham was 75 years old, God told him, "To your offspring I will give this land." (Genesis 12:7). Yet, Abraham had no offspring. God repeated this promise of an offspring in Genesis 13:15. Abraham said to God in Genesis 15:2 that he had no offspring but God asked him to look to the stars and know that counting his offspring would be like counting the stars. Abraham believed God, and God counted it to him as righteousness (Genesis 15:5-6).

However, Abraham remained childless. Because of Sarah's inability to conceive, Abraham and Sarah agreed that Abraham would have sex with Hagar, Sarah's servant, so that Sarah could have children through Hagar. Although Hagar bore Ishmael to Abraham (Genesis 16:1-16) when Abraham was 85 years old, Ishmael was not the offspring God purposed, for the offspring God wanted would come through His promise rather than through the flesh (Galatians 4:23). Therefore, when Abraham was 99 years old God promised an offspring again, this time through Sarah (Genesis 17:16). Abraham seemed to think such would be impossible and said to God, "Oh that Ishmael might live before you!" Abraham was 100 years old when Isaac was finally born to Abraham and Sarah (Genesis 21:5). Evidently Abraham had finally trusted God to bring about what He had promised.

God was not through with His formation of persistent faith and faithfulness in Abraham. In Genesis 22, God commanded Abraham to sacrifice his son Isaac, and this must have shaken the very soul of Abraham. Nevertheless, Abraham was completely obedient to God and took Isaac to the mountain in the land of Moriah to sacrifice Isaac as God had commanded. When Abraham had prepared Isaac for sacrifice, he reached for his knife to kill Isaac. However, God then intervened:

> [15] Then the angel of the LORD called to Abraham a second time from heaven, [16] and said, "By Myself I have sworn, declares the LORD, because you have done this thing and have not withheld your son, your only son, [17] indeed I will greatly bless you, and I will greatly multiply your seed as the stars of the heavens, and as the sand which is on the seashore; and your seed shall possess the gate of their enemies. [18] In your seed all the nations of the earth shall be blessed, because you have obeyed My voice." Genesis 22:15-18 (NASB)

There is every reason to believe that Abraham lived and died in a faithful relationship with God (Genesis 26:5).

Therefore, we must understand that God is sovereign, preeminent, and indisputable. He knows all things and has all power. Yet God has taken action and will continue to take action with the family of man to bring us to real faith in Him and real faithfulness to Him. The popular saying, "God is not finished with me yet," is a very true statement. Yet, if we don't get our answer to prayer today or tomorrow, will we continue in constant prayer? Will we be like those to whom Hebrews was written, who struggled with faith because of inconveniences, and spiritually had "drooping hands" and "weak knees" (Hebrews 12:12)? Or will we stand firmly in our faith despite what Satan tries to do to destroy our faith? Let Abraham be an example to us of real faith and faithfulness to God.

God Himself renewed and restored the covenant He made with Abraham, with **Isaac** (Genesis 26:1-5, 24) and **Jacob** (Genesis 28:12-15). Abraham's beloved son Isaac was a man who didn't struggle with God. This is best seen in what must have been his passive role as a sacrifice to God (Genesis 22:1-14). Isaac lived faithfully, though he was not perfect.

In contrast to Abraham and Isaac, Isaac's son **Jacob** truly struggled with God in his spiritual journey. He was complicit with his mother in misleading his blind father, Isaac, so that Isaac gave the blessing of the first-born to Jacob instead of Esau. Consequently Jacob paid dearly for this deception because he had to work 20 years for Laban who was a lying, misleading, and manipulating person, and who was so full of avarice that he changed Jacob's wages at least 10 times (Genesis 31:7). It appears that Jacob finally learned God's principle that we must reap what we have sown (Galatians 6:7). When Jacob returned to the land of his father, Isaac, he seemed to be a changed man, for he was humble toward Esau and pleaded with God to help him as he met his brother whom he had cheated. That night before he passed over the Jabbok, he wrestled with a man all night. The man dislocated Jacob's hip, but did not prevail over him. The message from God was very plain:

> [26] Then he said, "Let me go, for the dawn is breaking." But he said, "I will not let you go unless you bless me." [27] So he said to him, "What is your name?" And he said, "Jacob." [28] He said, "Your name shall no longer be Jacob, but Israel; for you have striven with God and with men and have prevailed." Genesis 32:26-28 (NASB)

Yet even after this Jacob continued to struggle with his faith, for he tolerated idolatry in his family until God spoke to him again in Genesis 35. Unfortunately, idolatry was present with the descendents of Jacob for centuries after this. Perhaps if Jacob had taken a firm stand against idolatry that would have made a difference for his descendents. Jacob had to endure the rape of his daughter Dinah (Genesis 34), the death of Rachel (Genesis 35:16-21), the incest of his first-born son Reuben (Genesis 35:22), his belief that Joseph, his favorite son, had been killed by a fierce animal (Genesis 37:33), and the death of Leah (Genesis 49:31). However, in spite of his many trials, or perhaps because of his many trials, the picture of Jacob at the end of his life was one of patient confidence in and faithful commitment to God. The Hebrew writer records this about Jacob near the end of his life:

> [21] By faith Jacob, as he was dying, blessed each of the sons of Joseph, and worshiped, leaning on the top of his staff. Hebrews 11:21 (NASB) (see also Genesis 47:31)

Therefore, we again find the manifestation of the grace of God. Because of His covenant relationship with Abraham, even after Abraham's death, God chose to continue to work with the double-minded grandson of Abraham—that is, Jacob. His work was not in vain because God's plan moved forward according to His divine will.

The Israelite Cultural Restoration of the Land Promise

In the times after the patriarchs, Abraham, Isaac, and Jacob (i.e., after Genesis), God's Covenant with Abraham is mentioned 42 times in the remainder of the Old Testament. This covenant was the fundamental reason God delivered the Israelites out of Egyptian captivity (Exodus 2:24) and led them to the land of Canaan (Deuteronomy 1:8). Moses used God's Covenant with Abraham, Isaac, and Jacob as one of the major reasons God should not destroy the idolatrous Israelites at Mount Sinai (Deuteronomy 9:27). God's Covenant with Abraham, Isaac, and Jacob was the primary reason why God promised to "remember the land" and bring the repentant Israelites out of captivity in other nations back to the land of Israel (Leviticus 26:40-45). Clearly, there was an emphasis in the Old Testament upon the "land promise" portion of God's Covenant with Abraham. Therefore, the Israelites never lost sight of the "land promise," and therefore, their faith in this particular benefit was constantly restored.

However, it appears that the Israelites did not give adequate consideration to the steadfast faith and faithfulness of Abraham, especially to his steadfast belief in the One and Only God of heaven and earth. Rather, they turned to idolatry, and this was the primary cause for the Assyrian destruction of the Northern ten tribes in 721 B.C., and it was also the primary cause of the Babylonian destruction of Judah and Jerusalem in 586 B.C. Had they treasured the faith and faithfulness of the patriarchs as much as the "land promise," they surely would have kept the land of Israel as their own precious possession.

Restoration of God's Covenant with Abraham by Christ's Apostles

In the New Testament, Abraham is mention 70 times. However, the emphasis is not on the "land promise" as it was in the Old Testament passages. Rather, the emphasis was made clear in Peter's second sermon:

> [25] "It is you who are the sons of the prophets and of the covenant which God made with your fathers, saying to Abraham, 'AND IN YOUR SEED ALL THE FAMILIES OF THE EARTH SHALL BE BLESSED.' Acts 3:25 (NASB)

Thus, God's Covenant with Abraham took on new life in Christ, who is the promised One in whom "all the families of the earth shall be blessed." This understanding of God's Covenant with Abraham gave great strength to Christian world evangelism, that is, not just to Jews, but to all the peoples and nations of the earth, as promised in God's covenant with Abraham. The apostle Paul summarized the shift in understanding this covenant as follows:

> [9] Is this blessing then upon the circumcised, or upon the uncircumcised also? For we say, "FAITH WAS CREDITED TO ABRAHAM

> AS RIGHTEOUSNESS." [10] How then was it credited? While he was circumcised, or uncircumcised? Not while circumcised, but while uncircumcised; [11] and he received the sign of circumcision, a seal of the righteousness of the faith which he had while uncircumcised, that he might be the father of all who believe without being circumcised, that righteousness might be reckoned to them, [12] and the father of circumcision to those who not only are of the circumcision, but who also follow in the steps of the faith of our father Abraham which he had while uncircumcised. Romans 4:9-12 (NASB)

Notice how Paul reaches back to stress the faith of Abraham instead of the "land promise." Again in Romans 4:16, Paul stresses that we must share the faith of Abraham, "who is the father of us all." Therefore, Paul calls believers in Christ, whether Jew or Gentile, "children of Abraham" (Romans 9:6-8). Again in Galatians, Paul writes,

> [7] Therefore, be sure that it is those who are of faith who are sons of Abraham. Galatians 3:7 (NASB)

Therefore, the New Testament again puts the spotlight on God's Covenant with Abraham by stressing the universal application of it for all peoples in all places and all times, and by stressing faith as the essential element in this covenant. The "land promise" had finished—God had given the land of Israel to the Jews, but they had repeatedly broken covenant with Him. Therefore, in 70 A.D. the Romans utterly destroyed Jerusalem and Judah, including their marvelous Temple just as Christ had prophesied, and this brought a complete end to the Jewish sacrificial system. The whole economy of what it meant to be a Jew vanished. Their land was incorporated into other nations, and Israel as a political and physical entity was utterly demolished.

In summary, let us as Christians therefore understand God's Covenant with Abraham. We must understand that the basis of our involvement in this covenant is faith, that is, the faith and faithfulness of Abraham. If we have the kind of faith that Abraham possessed, then we are the children of Abraham. Then we also share in all the benefits of Abraham who is the father of the faithful (Luke 16:19-31). Let us also understand that these benefits must be offered to all people in all places, that they also may become children of Abraham through having the faith of Abraham. Yes, just as the apostles did, so we also must restore this element of the steadfast and obedient faith of Abraham even for today because it is an essential portion of what is called Christianity.

Study Questions

1. What are the characteristics of Bible Covenants?
2. What are the covenants God has made with man?
3. What were the consequences of Adam's disobedience for himself and for all people?
4. What are the basic expectations of God regarding all people?
5. What is the first prophecy about Christ in the Bible?
6. What would have happened if Noah refused to build the ark or Abraham refused circumcision?
7. In what way are the ark and flood symbolic in our own salvation?
8. Is there a contradiction between Paul and James regarding how we are justified?
9. What is the basis of Abraham's relationship with God?
10. How did God work over decades to increase Abraham's faith?
11. How did God restore the covenant with Abraham?
12. Is God's covenant with Abraham restored in some way for Christians today? How?

Chapter 2

Mosaic Covenant: Moses to Solomon

When God made a covenant with Israel, Moses was the intermediary. Therefore the covenant is often called the Mosaic Law. David Lusk has described the salient points of this covenant, to which I have added "Blessings and Curses" as follows:

1. Preamble/Historical Prologue (Exodus 19:1-4)
2. Invitation (Exodus 19:5-6)
3. Terms of the Covenant (Exodus 20-23)
4. Blessings and Curses (Deuteronomy 27-28; Numbers 15:30-31)
5. Ratification of the Covenant, with blood (Exodus 24)
6. Sign of the Covenant—Sabbath (Exodus 31:13-17)
7. Storage of the Covenant (Deuteronomy 31:24-26)
8. The Covenant Meal (Exodus 24:9-11) (Lusk, 1994, pp. 54-56)

It is important to realize that all of God's mighty acts of deliverance that resulted in the Israelites' exodus from Egyptian slavery were all completed prior to this covenant. Therefore, God delivered them out of slavery by His grace and not by their works of righteousness and uprightness. In fact, He delivered them out of slavery because of His promise to Abraham, Isaac, and Jacob (Exodus 2:24; 6:8; Deuteronomy 9:5).

However, the Israelites had become deeply steeped in idolatry during their stay in Egypt. They carried their idols with them when they came out of Egypt (Amos 5:25-26; Acts 7:42-43) (Hailey, 1993, p. 112). They openly demonstrated their idolatry when Moses went up on the mountain to receive the Law (Exodus 32:1-6). They did this even after seeing how God overthrew Egypt with the ten plagues and parted the Red Sea so they could pass on dry ground. They did this even though they saw God overthrow Pharaoh and his army by causing the Red Sea to come down upon them. Except for their lineage to the Patriarchs, there was nothing about them that would make them worthy of God's favor. Therefore, they were saved by God's grace and mercy and because He is a covenant-keeping God who remembered His promises to the Patriarchs. Only after these dramatic acts of deliverance did God give them the Mosaic Law so that they would understand how they should live before the King of the Universe, the God of Abraham, Isaac, and Jacob. Thus, God Himself restored the covenant He made with the Patriarchs when He delivered their offspring from bondage and gave their offspring the land of Israel.

Some Gentiles think they are under the Mosaic Law in this present time. However, the place of Gentiles prior to salvation by Christ is best described by Paul as follows:

> [11] Therefore remember that formerly you, the Gentiles in the flesh, who are called "Uncircumcision" by the so-called "Circumcision," which is performed in the flesh by human hands— [12] remember that you were at that time separate from Christ, excluded from the commonwealth of Israel, and strangers to the covenants of promise, having no hope and without God in the world. Ephesians 2:11-12 (NASB)

But thanks be to God, Paul continues in Ephesians 2:13-22 to show that the only hope for us is in Christ Jesus our Lord.

We will now consider the restorations of God's Covenant with Israel through Moses.

Moses as a Restorer of the Mosaic Covenant (1447-1407 BC)

Just as Moses read the Book of the Covenant to the people in Exodus 24:7, he commanded it to be read at the Feast of Booths every seven years (Deuteronomy 31:10-11). Thus Moses put into effect a method of restoring the Mosaic Law to the people on a regular basis. Indeed, the Mosaic Law was also renewed and restored by Moses in Deuteronomy to a new generation of Jews. This generation of Jews had not been circumcised during their wilderness wanderings. Moses retold the teachings and the events of Exodus, Leviticus, and Numbers. As Lusk shows, this retelling of the Law can be outlined as follows:

1. Preamble (Deuteronomy 1:1-5)
2. Historical prologue (Deuteronomy 1:6 to 3:29)
3. Terms of the Covenant (Deuteronomy 4:1 to 26:19)
4. Blessings and Curses (Deuteronomy 27:1 to 30:20)
5. Disposition (Deuteronomy 31:1 to 34:12) (modified from Lusk, 1994, pp. 107-108)

Neither God nor Moses assumed that this new generation of Jews adequately understood the Mosaic Covenant. Therefore, this event must teach us that we can never assume that the job of restoring the New Covenant can ever be finished. At the very least, it must be given to every new generation again and again or they will cease to know or understand the New Covenant. If Moses commanded that Deuteronomy be read to all people at the end of every seven years, surely we should be reading the New Covenant to all the members of the church more often than that. Unfortunately, few Christians are daily Bible readers.

We should also recognize that God commanded through Moses the following regarding Jewish kings:

> [18] "Now it shall come about when he sits on the throne of his kingdom, he shall write for himself a copy of this law on a scroll in the presence of the Levitical priests. [19] It shall be with him and he shall read it all the days of his life, that he may learn to fear

> the LORD his God, by carefully observing all the words of this law and these statutes, [20] that his heart may not be lifted up above his countrymen and that he may not turn aside from the commandment, to the right or the left; so that he and his sons may continue long in his kingdom in the midst of Israel." Deuteronomy 17:18-20 (NASB)

Church leaders, please hearken to God's wisdom and read for yourselves daily the New Covenant. Then read, renew, and restore the New Covenant to all Christians. If not, we will fall away from the New Covenant just as the Jews fell away from their Mosaic Covenant.

Joshua as a Restorer of the Mosaic Covenant (1407-1385 BC)

The LORD strongly charged Joshua to be faithful to the Mosaic Covenant in Joshua 1:7-8. All evidence indicates that Joshua was faithful in all these things for his whole life.

In Joshua 8:30-31, after the fall of Ai, Joshua built an altar on Mount Ebal just as the LORD had commanded in the Book of the Law. At that time Joshua wrote copies of the Law of Moses on stones (Joshua 8:32). Then Joshua read the whole law to the people:

> [34] Then afterward he read all the words of the law, the blessing and the curse, according to all that is written in the book of the law. [35] There was not a word of all that Moses had commanded which Joshua did not read before all the assembly of Israel with the women and the little ones and the strangers who were living among them. Joshua 8:34-35 (NASB)

Much later Joshua renewed the Mosaic Covenant at Shechem (Joshua 24:1-27). A modified outline of this renewal from Lusk is as follows:

1. Historical Prologue (Joshua 24:1-13)
2. Invitation to the Covenant (Joshua 24:14-15)
3. Response of the Jews (Joshua 24:16-18)

4. Blessings and Curses (Joshua 24:19-21)
5. Terms (Joshua 24:22-24)
6. Memorial (Joshua 24:26-27) (Lusk, 1994, p. 108)

It should be noted that Joshua made it very clear which covenant he was renewing (Joshua 24:26). Therefore, Joshua was a very faithful restorer of the Mosaic Covenant. He is an example to us that we need to faithfully restore the New Covenant.

Also, just as Joshua faithfully read the Book of the Law to the people as Moses had commanded, we also must never get tired of reading the New Covenant to the church. Just as Paul charged Timothy, we must devote ourselves to the public reading of Scripture (1 Timothy 4:13). Paul commanded Timothy to follow the apostolic teachings:

> [13] <u>Retain the standard of sound words</u> which you have heard from me, in the faith and love which are in Christ Jesus. [14] Guard, through the Holy Spirit who dwells in us, the treasure which has been entrusted to you. 2 Timothy 1:13-14 (NASB)

Paul further charged Timothy to pass these apostolic teachings on to faithful men who would teach others also (2 Timothy 2:1-2). We surely are charged to do this also. If we refuse, then we are not the faithful men who are to pass on these apostolic teachings.

The Judges as Restorers of God's Mosaic Covenant (1385-1050 BC)

The Jews after Joshua's generation did not continue the never-ending work of restoring the Mosaic Covenant. Therefore, we find out in Judges 2:10 what happened because of this neglect:

> [10] And all that generation also were gathered to their fathers; and there arose another generation after them who did not know the LORD, nor yet the work which He had done for Israel. Judges 2:10 (NASB)

As a consequence of these Jews not knowing the LORD and what He had done for Israel, the Mosaic Covenant was lost to the knowledge of the Jews, and everyone did "what was right in his own eyes" (Judges 17:6; 21:25). This action by the Jews was a direct violation of Deuteronomy 12:8.

These Jews abandoned God and instead of serving the LORD, they bowed down to the Baals and the Ashtaroth. These were the idols/gods of the people surrounding them, and the Jews succumbed to the illusion of peace that comes from not being the distinctive people of God. As a result, they broke covenant with God, and multiple cycles followed as described in the book of Judges:

1. The people forsook the Lord.
2. God punished them by raising up a foreign power to oppress them.
3. The people cried out to God for deliverance.
4. The Lord raised up a deliverer for them.

These deliverers were the "Judges" that the biblical book is named after.

It is obvious that God, through the Judges, was trying to bring the Israelites back to the Mosaic Covenant. However, the Jews appeared to be hard-headed, stiff-necked, and two-faced in their dealings with God. Nevertheless, God's great patience for the Jews for their more than 300 years of double-mindedness is manifested greatly in God not completely destroying them.

In total, there were 15 judges who served as deliverers. Thirteen are recorded in Judges, and two are recorded in 1 Samuel. These are as follows:

1. Othniel (Judges 3:7-11)
2. Ehud (Judges 3:12-30)
3. Shamgar (Judges 3:31)
4. Deborah (Judges 4:1 to 5:31)
5. Barak (Judges 4:1 to 5:31)
6. Gideon (Judges 6:1 to 8:35)
7. Tola (Judges 10:1-2)
8. Jair (Judges 10:3-5)
9. Jephthah (Judges 11:1 to 12:7)

10. Ibzan (Judges 12:8-10)
11. Elon (Judges 12:11-12)
12. Abdon (Judges 12:13-15)
13. Samson (Judges 13:1 to 16:31)
14. Eli (1 Samuel 1:3-4:18)
15. Samuel (1 Samuel 1:20 to 25:1; and see 1 Samuel 7:15)

It should be noted that Samuel also appointed his sons as Judges (1 Samuel 8:1), but they did evil and the Israelites did not accept them.

Unfortunately, each time God delivered the Jews from their oppressors by one of the Judges, the Jews again refused to listen to the Judges and so fell back into idolatry. Thus, they repeatedly broke covenant with the LORD (Judges 2:16-17). The pattern in Judges is unmistakable. Clearly, it was God who wanted so much for His people to return to the covenant relationship He had graciously bestowed upon their fathers through Moses. Yet, they refused. He called and called and called, but they would only call upon Him for help when their dead idols couldn't provide for their acute needs. Their desire to be like the nations around them was far greater than their desire to be the unique people of the LORD.

The Judges realized who they were and understood it was God who was trying to restore the covenant relationship with his people. Gideon understood all the good that God had done for His people (Judges 6:13). When the people wanted Gideon to rule over them, he said,

> [22] Then the men of Israel said to Gideon, "Rule over us, both you and your son, also your son's son, for you have delivered us from the hand of Midian." [23] But Gideon said to them, "I will not rule over you, nor shall my son rule over you; the LORD shall rule over you." Judges 8:22-23 (NASB)

Therefore, what marks the book of Judges is the extreme duplicity of the Israelites. They called out to God for help to meet their acute needs, but then turned back to their idols when the crisis had passed. This recurring pattern continued over a considerable time, possibly 300 or more years. This shows God's incredible patience toward the descendents of Abraham. Athough they deserved destruction, God sustained them.

Perhaps the reason for God's incredible patience was that there continued to be a few who lived their lives faithfully to God regardless of what blessing or trouble came their way. Certainly the book of Ruth reflects the period of the Judges (Ruth 1:1). Naomi and Ruth are examples of steadfast faith surviving even in the most extreme troubles of life. Many of the Judges were clearly godly people. The parents of Samson were also godly people. In fact, one godly person can save an entire people from destruction:

> [30] "And I searched for a man among them who should build up the wall and stand in the gap before Me for the land, that I should not destroy it; but I found no one. [31] Thus I have poured out My indignation on them; I have consumed them with the fire of My wrath; their way I have brought upon their heads," declares the Lord GOD. Ezekiel 22:30-31 (NASB) (see also Isaiah 59:16; Jeremiah 5:1)

The last judge called by God was Samuel (1 Samuel 3). He emphasized the stark contrast between the Lord and the idols of the Jews. He was effective in restoring the Jewish people to God (1 Samuel 7:3-4). Samuel knew his own people well and understood the Mosaic Covenant God had with them. Just as Joshua did, so Samuel also called the people and gave them the same kind of exhortation in his farewell address (1 Samuel 12).

The point is this: If God continued steadfastly to restore those Jews to the Mosaic Covenant for over 300 years, should we not also try to restore the New Covenant in our own day and never give up? Will we restore what God has given us in the New Covenant, or will we be happy with 1900 years worth of unauthorized teachings of men which have supplanted the New Testament teachings among so many people?

King David as a Restorer of the Mosaic Covenant (Reigned 1010-970 BC)

Although God made a special covenant with the House of David, King David himself was a most zealous restorer of the Mosaic Covenant.

David made his mistakes, his sins, his blunders, for he was like any man who had ever lived past the innocence of childhood.

However, God chose David, and said,

> [22] After He had removed him, He raised up David to be their king, concerning whom He also testified and said, "I HAVE FOUND DAVID the son of Jesse, A MAN AFTER MY HEART, who will do all My will." Acts 13:22-23 (NASB) (see also 1 Samuel 13:14)

Indeed, God's choice of David involved His choice for Israel His people:

> [10] I will also appoint a place for My people Israel and will plant them, that they may live in their own place and not be disturbed again, nor will the wicked afflict them any more as formerly. 2 Samuel 7:10 (NASB)

Now let us consider what David did to restore the Mosaic Covenant. First, he brought the Ark to Jerusalem. His first attempt was in ignorance, and God struck Uzzah dead for touching the Ark (1 Chronicles 13). But when David successfully brought the Ark to Jerusalem later (1 Chronicles 15), he did so with full knowledge and application of God's commands as found in the Mosaic Covenant (Numbers 4:15; 1 Chronicles 15:12-15). David at first was angered at God and fearful of God because of God's judgment on Uzzah (1 Chronicles 13:11-12). However, he went back to the covenant and corrected his ignorance and then did exactly what the Lord had commanded Moses.

Not only this, but David also organized worship before the Ark of the Covenant (1 Chronicles 16:4-7, 37-42) and this included the continual morning and evening burnt offerings, "... even according to all that is written in the Law of the Lord, which He commanded Israel." (1 Chronicles 16:40; Exodus 29:38-42; Numbers 28:3-4). David also restored the offerings to the Lord on "Sabbaths, new moons and feast days." David organized the priests and Levites (1 Chronicles 23:2-24) as well as the musicians (1 Chronicles 25), the gatekeepers (1 Chronicles 26), and the treasurers and other officials (1 Chronicles 26). Thus, elements of the

Jewish worship according to the Law of Moses were observed (2 Chronicles 29:25). Therefore, it appears that David did a rather thorough job of restoring the Mosaic Covenant.

David had a great desire to build a house for the LORD. However, God said David's son would build it (1 Chronicles 17:11-12), and Solomon did built the Temple. However, David prepared for the Temple by stockpiling great quantities of building materials for Solomon's use (1 Chronicles 22).

In addition to these widespread restorations of Jewish worship according to the Law of Moses, 73 of the 150 Psalms are attributed to David. Therefore, David had a permanent impact on the religious expression of the Jewish people throughout their generations. Truly, David was a zealous restorer of the Mosaic Covenant. As testified by God, David's heart was in the right place.

What David accomplished in restoring the Mosaic Covenant was remarkable. We should consider what had been done before him. Although Moses commanded the reading of the Law every seven years (Deuteronomy 31:10-11), it appears unlikely that this practice was done past the time of Joshua. This means that during the approximate 300 years of the judges, no such public readings of the Law by the priests and Levites were done because the people had turned to idols and no longer knew God. This was the "Dark Ages" for the Jews. When David came along 300 years later, he restored what he could. However, he was a warrior king and not a priest or a Levite. To do all he did, including the Psalms he wrote during his time, was remarkable indeed.

May God grant that each one of us will be to God as David was—that is, a man or woman after God's own heart, who will do all of God's will. Let us have the same zeal as David to restore the New Covenant of our Lord and Savior Jesus Christ.

King Solomon as a Restorer of the Mosaic Covenant (Reigned 970-930 BC)

Regarding faithfulness to God, Solomon started well but ended badly. As a new King, he was very young (1 Kings 3:7), probably younger than 18 years old (Robinson, 1939, 1956). However, he had the humility to ask for wisdom from God. Because of this, God chose also to bless him with riches and honor (1 Kings 3:3-14). Truly, Solomon did love the Lord when he was young.

As a restorer of the Mosaic Covenant, Solomon's chief contribution was what his father King David as well as God Almighty had assigned him: To build the Temple (1 Kings 6:1-38; 7:13-51; 2 Chronicles 2:1 to 5:1). Solomon's prayer for the dedication of the Temple is very moving (1 Kings 8:22-66). However, the Temple was not a requirement of the Mosaic Covenant. Rather, it was David's desire—since he lived in a very nice house, shouldn't God have a house of cedar also? Yet, God had been enthroned above the mercy seat in a tent for about 400 years and He had never commanded anyone to build him a house (2 Samuel 7:4-7). However, God did accept the Temple built by Solomon, and indwelled it (1 Kings 8:10-11).

The Temple took on a special significance for the Jews, and it would be a vivid part of their tradition for 1000 years. Unfortunately, the Temple's predominate significance was physical rather than spiritual. What God wanted was a house of prayer (Isaiah 56:7), but the Jews made it a den of robbers (Jeremiah 7:11). This same behavior recurred in the Temple Herod built (Matthew 21:13). In the centuries after the Temple was built by Solomon, every abomination would be brought into the Temple and made part of the "worship" (2 Kings 23:7; Ezekiel 8). King Ahaz even shut the doors of the Temple because he was completely devoted to idolatry (2 Chronicles 28:22-24). The Temple that Solomon built was destroyed in 586 BC when, in the third deportation, Babylon destroyed Jerusalem. This was the LORD's will because of the Jew's persistent idolatry and related sins.

Unfortunately, Solomon abandoned God in his later years because of his foreign wives and followed them into idolatry (1 Kings 11:4-8). His unfaithfulness to God was the proximal cause of God abolishing the monarchy and splitting the kingdom into the Northern and Southern kingdoms. So why mention Solomon at all? Solomon, by his early leadership, gave generous gifts and showed a good example. During this period Solomon surely encouraged many to devote themselves to God when he was young. Two of the Psalms (72, 127), Proverbs, Ecclesiastes, and the Song of Solomon are all attributed to Solomon and are part of the Holy Scriptures. Solomon was very wise, and we have much to learn from reading the wisdom God gave to him. When Solomon was true to God, surely he helped restore the Mosaic Covenant.

Yet another reason for mentioning Solomon is that his case demonstrates that God is no respecter of persons. God laid down the Law with Moses concerning kings in Israel (Deuteronomy 17:14-20), and Solomon openly violated every aspect of that law. This is illustrated in the following five points:

1. God said that the King must not acquire many horses, but Solomon did (1 Kings 4:26; 10:26, 28; 2 Chronicles 1:16; 9:28; Isaiah 31:1).
2. God said that neither the King nor the people were to go back to Egypt to get horses, but Solomon did (see above and also Ezekiel 17:15).
3. God said the King must not multiply wives, but Solomon did—700 wives and princesses and 300 concubines. "And his wives turned away his heart." (1 Kings 11:2-4; Nehemiah 13:26). Many of these were foreign, pagan wives which God prohibited (Exodus 34:11-16).
4. God said the King must not multiply silver and gold, but Solomon did (1 Kings 10:14, 27).
5. God said the King must write for himself a copy of the Law "... and read it all the days of his life" (Deuteronomy 17:18-20). If Solomon would have done this, he most likely would not have turned away from God.

God was exceedingly clear with Solomon that His blessings on Solomon and his lineage were conditional (1 Kings 9:4-9), and would be withdrawn if Solomon did not keep His commands, statutes, and rules. God Himself appeared to Solomon twice (1 Kings 3:5-14; 9:2-9). Yet in spite of this incredible privilege, Solomon violated every command God gave to Kings in the Law of Moses. His pagan wives turned away his heart from God, and he turned away from God in order to worship the Ashtoreth, Milcom, Chemosh, and Molech—all gods of his pagan wives. He also built temples for these gods (1 Kings 11:1-8). God's displeasure, rebuke and punishment for these things are found in 1 Kings 11:9-40.

Therefore, no matter how rich or poor or powerful or beautiful we are, God is no respecter of persons. "The soul who sins shall die" (see Ezekiel 18). The accounts of Solomon show no evidence of repentance in his old age. He must stand before God knowing that by his example in his old age, he caused many to fall from the covenant relationship with God. He died without renouncing his love affair with idols and all his related sins.

Study Questions

1. Were the Israelites idolaters while in Egypt? Were they idolaters after the miraculous 10 plagues God brought upon the Egyptians and their gods? Were they idolaters after the miraculous crossing of the Red Sea? Were they idolaters during the giving of the Mosaic Covenant on Mount Sinai?
2. Why did God deliver the Israelites out of Egyptian captivity and put up with their idolatry?
3. Prior to Mt Sinai, did God save them by His grace or by their righteous works?
4. Explain the "curse of the Law" and how Christians are delivered from this (Deuteronomy 27:26; Galatians 3:10-14).
5. What was the purpose of the Mosaic Law (Galatians 3:19; 23-27)?
6. Are we under the Mosaic Law today (Romans 10:4)?
7. Was the Mosaic Law inspired by God (2 Timothy 3:16)?
8. Is the Mosaic Law useful in Christian teachings today (1 Timothy 1:8-11; 2 Timothy 3:15)?
9. Show how the following people restored the Mosaic Covenant: Moses, Joshua, the Judges, King David, and King Solomon.
10. How often did Moses command that the Book of the Covenant be read to all the people?
11. The kings were commanded to write their own copy of the Law in the presence of the Levitical priests. How often were the kings commanded to read this copy?

12. How often do you read your Bible? How often does God want you to read your Bible? How often should the Bible be read to the church? (1 Timothy 4:13)

Chapter 3

Mosaic Covenant: Asa to the Prophets

King Asa as a Restorer of the Mosaic Covenant (Reigned 910-869 BC)

The accounts of King Asa are found in 1 Kings 15:9-24 and 2 Chronicles 14:1 to 16:14. Conditions at the time of King Asa are described in 2 Chronicles 15:3. For a long time, Israel was without the true God, and without a teaching priest and without law. After King David, Asa was the next king about whom it was said, "And Asa did what was right in the eyes of the LORD, as David his father had done" (1 Kings 15:11). It is remarkable that such deterioration could occur in just 20 years. Asa did the following in his effort to restore the Mosaic Covenant:

1. He removed the male and female cult prostitutes.
2. He removed all the idols his fathers had made.
3. He removed his mother from being the queen mother since she worshipped Asherah.
4. He brought sacred gifts into the House of the LORD.
5. He commanded Judah to seek the LORD, the God of their fathers, and to keep the Law and the commandments (2 Chronicles 14:4).
6. "The people entered into a covenant to seek the Lord, the God

of their fathers, with all their heart and with all their soul" (2 Chronicles 15:12). The people swore an oath to God (2 Chronicles 15:14).

However, Asa made mistakes in that he took actions that were contrary to the Mosaic Covenant. These included the following:

1. He made a covenant with Ben-hadad, king of Syria (1 Kings 15:18-21). (see also Exodus 23:32; Deuteronomy 7:2).
2. He jailed a prophet who rebuked him for making this covenant (2 Chronicles 16:7-10).
3. He did not remove the high places (2 Chronicles 15:17).
4. He did not seek the LORD when he became ill (2 Chronicles 16:12).

Therefore, Asa tried to restore the Mosaic Covenant. He made mistakes, some of which were very serious. But his heart was "wholly true all his days." (2 Chronicles 15:17)

King Jehoshaphat as a Restorer of the Mosaic Covenant (Reigned 872-848 BC)

The account of King Jehoshaphat is found in 1 Kings 22:41-50 and 2 Chronicles 17 to 20. His efforts to restore the Mosaic Covenant are as follows:

1. He walked in the way of King Asa his father (1 Kings 22:43).
2. He sought and walked in His commandments (2 Chronicles 17:4).
3. He was courageous in the ways of the Lord (2 Chronicles 17:6).
4. He made initial efforts to take away the high places and the Asherim out of Judah (2 Chronicles 17:6).
5. He sent his officials with priests and Levites to teach the Book of the Law of the Lord to the people in Judah (2 Chronicles 17:7-9).
6. He went out to all the people and brought them back to the Lord. Thus, King Jehoshaphat was evangelistic (2 Chronicles 19:4).
7. He appointed judges and told them to judge not for man but for

the LORD (2 Chronicles 19:5-7).

8. He appointed Levites and priests to judge for the LORD and charged them to fear God (2 Chronicles 19:8-11).
9. He cried out to God publicly for deliverance from the armies of the Moabites, Ammonites, Edomites and Mennites, and God granted his request (2 Chronicles 20).

However, King Jehoshaphat was not perfect, and he did things that were against the Mosaic Covenant as follows:

1. He joined forces with Ahab in the form of a marriage alliance (2 Chronicles 18:1).
2. He was not able to destroy completely the high places because the people would not agree (2 Chronicles 20:33; 1 Kings 22:43).
3. He ignored the prophet who warned Ahab (2 Chronicles 18:12-22) and went out with Ahab to fight the king of Syria. Jehoshaphat was rebuked by another prophet in Judah for the same thing (2 Chronicles 19:1-3). Because the Northern ten tribes worshipped idols, they were regarded as unbelievers by God.
4. He joined with Ahaziah, the son of Ahab, in a commercial ship-building venture, but Ahaziah was wicked. Jehoshaphat was rebuked by a prophet for this also (2 Chronicles 20:37).

Jehoshaphat evidently was a joiner and not a splitter. He had his own "ecumenical movement" with efforts to influence and join with his idolatrous Jewish "brothers," Kings Ahab and Ahaziah. So intent was he to succeed with Ahab that he even ignored prophetic guidance and correction, and nearly died as a result. He tried again with Ahaziah, Ahab's son, in a commercial for-profit business. However, he was rebuked by God's prophet again. In both instances he was trying to yoke himself with unbelievers who were related to him by blood.

Therefore, Jehoshaphat was a good king, but had certain failings. That he did not turn to idols made the good outweigh the bad. This good king Jehoshaphat teaches us three important lessons:

1. Love the LORD with all your heart, soul, mind and strength (Luke 10:27).

2. Be evangelistic in your efforts to restore the New Covenant (Matthew 28:18-20).
3. Do not be unequally yoked with unbelievers (2 Corinthians 6:14), even if they are your distant relatives, or God will rebuke you (2 Chronicles 19:1-3).

King Joash & Priest Jehoiada as Restorers of the Mosaic Covenant (Joash Reigned 835-796 BC)

King Joash's history is recorded in 2 Kings 11:1 to 12:21 and 2 Chronicles 22:10 to 24:27. King Joash (Jehoash) was 7 years old when he began to reign, and he reigned for 40 years. His father Ahaziah was killed by Jehu, and his grandmother Athaliah then murdered all of Ahaziah's sons so she could reign. However, Jehosheba rescued one-year old Joash, son of Ahaziah, and he was hidden and raised in the House of the LORD for six years. In the seventh year, Jehoiada the priest convinced all the leaders to appoint Ahaziah's son Joash as King. Athaliah was killed. Jehoiada the priest made a covenant between the LORD, the king, and the people, that they should be the LORD's people, and also between the king and the people (2 Kings 11:17).

Jehoiada's immediate reforms were to destroy the house of Baal and the priest of Baal (2 Kings 11:18) and restore the sacrificial system according to the Law of Moses (2 Chronicles 23:18-19). King Joash did what was pleasing to God as long as Jehoiada the priest was living. King Joash repaired the Temple (2 Kings 12:4-16) which helped restore the Mosaic Law. However, after the death of Jehoiada the priest, King Joash was pressured by the influential princes of Judah, and he abandoned the House of the LORD and served Asherim and idols (2 Chronicles 24:17-19). King Joash then rejected the prophets God sent to him, and he even stoned the prophet Zechariah, who was the son of Jehoiada the priest, and who rebuked him for breaking the commandment of the LORD (2 Chronicles 24:20-22).

Therefore, the only good that King Joash did was to repair the Temple. It was Jehoiada the priest who restored the Mosaic Covenant.

Lessons we learn from this account are as follows:

1. If our faith is dependent on another person's faith, and we don't make that faith our own, then when that person dies our faith will die also. That's what happened to Joash. If your faith is because of a faithful father, mother, preacher, elder, or leader, you must make it your own or your faith will die when they die.
2. We should honor Jehoiada's and his son Zechariah's faith. They loved the LORD and were faithful unto death. They were the true restorers of the Mosaic Covenant.
3. We don't have to occupy some high office like president or senator to be a restorer of the New Covenant. We should live the New Covenant and share it so others will be influenced by it.

King Amaziah as a Restorer of the Mosaic Covenant (Reigned 797-767 BC)

The account of King Amaziah of Judah is found in 2 Kings 14:1-22 and 2 Chronicles 25:1-28. Amaziah was 25 years old when he began to reign, and he reigned 29 years. He was like his father Joash, and called a good king. Like his father he started his reign well, but he ended it poorly.

Amaziah killed the people who had murdered his father King Joash, but he did not kill their children because of what Moses commanded in Deuteronomy 24:16—

> 16 "Fathers shall not be put to death for their sons, nor shall sons be put to death for their fathers; everyone shall be put to death for his own sin. Deuteronomy 24:16 (NASB)

This was a striking example of a restoration of the Mosaic Law. 2 Kings 14:6 quotes this passage in Deuteronomy, saying it was written in the Book of the Law of Moses where the LORD commanded.

After this King Amaziah mustered his army in Judah and also hired 100,000 mighty men from Israel as well. One might suppose that this was his way of trying to reunite the broken family of Jacob. Certainly,

King Jehoshaphat had a great desire to do that also, but he was rebuked for it twice by the prophets of God. In the same way, King Amaziah was also rebuked by a man of God, but Amaziah listened and then sent the 100,000 mighty men from Israel back to their own place.

Amaziah then led a successful military campaign against Edom (2 Kings 14:7) and this should have reassured him that God would be with him if he followed God's commands. Instead, Amaziah brought the Edomite gods back and made them his own gods, thus rejecting the LORD. God sent him a prophet to correct him, but Amaziah refused to receive the correction this time (2 Chronicles 25:14-16).

Amaziah then picked a fight with King Joash, son of Jehoahaz. They fought, but King Joash of Israel defeated and captured King Amaziah of Judah. All this was from the LORD because Amaziah had sought the gods of Edom. Amaziah was later murdered (2 Chronicles 25:17-28).

Therefore, King Amaziah honored and restored the Mosaic Covenant by his actions toward the children of the murderers of his father Joash. This was a big step for Amaziah and it should not be underestimated. In addition, Amaziah was humble enough to receive correction by a man of God regarding the 100,000 mighty men he had hired from Israel. This correction was based on a similar sin of Jehoshaphat (2 Chronicles 19:1-3). The conclusion can only be that as long as the Northern ten tribes worshipped idols, they must be regarded as unbelievers; consequently there could be no marriages, treaties, or covenants made with them.

God granted Amaziah success until Amaziah decided he would forsake the LORD and serve the idols of Edom. This was clearly a poor choice on Amaziah's part because these Edomite gods were not able to save Edom from Amaziah's attack. Then God removed His blessing from Amaziah, which caused the defeat of Judah by Israel.

Some lessons learned from King Amaziah are as follows:

1. We must restore and obey the New Covenant even if it is inconvenient and even when it isn't what others "feel" is right for the times.
2. We must constantly study the New Covenant so we will see what is right and continue to do it.
3. If we abandon God, God will withdraw His blessing from us.
4. We should not pick fights with others.

5. We must not be unequally yoked with unbelievers (2 Chronicles 19:1-3; 2 Corinthians 6:14).

King Azariah as a Restorer of the Mosaic Covenant (Reigned 792-740 BC)

The account of King Azariah (Uzziah) is found in 2 Kings 15:1-7 and 2 Chronicles 26:1-23. He was 16 years old when he started to reign and reigned 52 years. Like King Amaziah, he started well but finished poorly. Like Joash, Uzziah had a religious instructor named Zechariah who instructed him in the fear of God. As long as Uzziah sought God, God prospered him. God helped King Uzziah in his military campaigns. The king improved facilities, both rural and urban. He had a large and well-equipped army of 307,500 men.

However, when he became strong, he also became proud and his pride was his undoing. He violated the Mosaic Law when he decided to enter the Temple and burn incense on the Altar of Incense. Azariah the priest and 80 other priests opposed him and reminded him of the Commandment in the Mosaic Law (Numbers 16:40; 18:7) that only Aaron and his sons were consecrated to burn incense. Uzziah became angry at this reprimand and immediately God struck him with leprosy. The priests rushed him out of the Temple and he lived separate as a leper until he died. As a leper, he could not even enter the Temple to worship God.

Again we find that God was with King Uzziah (Azariah) when King Uzziah was with God. When he abandoned God, God punished him severely, just as God had done with previous kings. The real restorers in this account were the faithful priests who, at great personal risk, restored the Mosaic Covenant regarding burning incense in the Temple.

From this account we learn the following:

1. God will be with us if we trust and obey Him.
2. If we turn our backs on God, He will punish us (Hebrews 6:6; 10:29; 2 Peter 2:20-22).
3. Pride is followed by disgrace (Proverbs 8:13; 11:2; 16:18; 29:23).
4. We must try to restore the New Covenant even if those in authority say we must stop.

5. We must have the courage to stand for God's word just like the 80 priests who withstood King Uzziah.

King Jotham as a Restorer of the Mosaic Covenant (Reigned 750-732 BC)

We learn of King Jotham in 2 Kings 15:32-38 and 2 Chronicles 27:1-9. King Jotham had charge of the government for about 10 years while his father, King Uzziah, lived as a leper. He started ruling when he was 25 years old. He did what was right in God's sight. However, the high places were not removed and the people were corrupt. His building projects and military campaigns were successful. Scripture says King Jotham "... ordered his ways before the LORD his God" and this was the reason God blessed him (2 Chronicles 27:6).

We learn the following from King Jotham:

1. We must not live careless lives, but must order our ways before the LORD our God.
2. By doing this, King Jotham restored the Mosaic Covenant.
3. To order our lives now is to pattern our lives after the teachings of the New Covenant.
4. If we do this, we will restore the New Covenant.
5. We must live the restored New Covenant personally. If we believe it and preach it but don't live it, we become hypocrites.

King Hezekiah as a Restorer of the Mosaic Covenant (Reigned 715-686 BC)

We learn of King Hezekiah in 2 Kings 18:1-20:21 and 2 Chronicles 29:1-32:33. King Hezekiah started reigning at 25 years of age and continued to reign in Judah until he was 54 years old. He was complemented by Scripture as doing what was right in the eyes of the LORD (2 Kings 18:3; 2 Chronicles 29:2; 31:20-21). He tried hard to undo the evil that his father, King Ahaz, had done. The following summarizes the life of this great restorer of the Mosaic Covenant:

1. Hezekiah removed all idolatry, including the high places (2 Kings 18:4).
2. Hezekiah opened the doors of the Temple and repaired them in the first year of his reign (2 Chronicles 29:3).
3. Hezekiah restored the priests and the Levites back to their service in the Temple (2 Chronicles 29:4-19).
4. Hezekiah restored the Temple worship (2 Chronicles 29:20-36).
5. Hezekiah restored the Passover (2 Chronicles 30:1-27).
6. King Hezekiah restored the organization of the priests (2 Chronicles 31:1-21).
7. Hezekiah restored the defenses of Jerusalem (2 Chronicles 32:3-5).
8. Hezekiah trusted God, and God delivered Jerusalem from the Assyrian army (2 Kings 18:13-37; 2 Chronicles 32:1-23).
9. Hezekiah trusted God and God saved him from a deadly sickness (2 Chronicles 32:24; 2 Kings 20:1-11).

King Hezekiah is truly a wonderful role model for us today. He was deeply committed to the LORD, and he worked with all his strength to do what was right in God's sight. We also see from King Hezekiah that just because a father is evil doesn't mean that his son must be evil also. We should be greatly encouraged by this account of King Hezekiah. Taking Hezekiah as our example, we should try with all of our might to restore the New Covenant during the time we have.

King Manasseh as a Restorer of the Mosaic Covenant (Reigned 697-642 BC)

We learn about King Manasseh in 2 Kings 21:1-18 and 2 Chronicles 33:1-20. King Manasseh was the son of King Hezekiah. He was 12 years old when he began to reign, and he reigned for 55 years in Jerusalem.

King Manasseh is not on the usual list of good Kings because he started his reign doing great evil. The following illustrates the evil that he did during his early reign:

1. He rebuilt the high places that Hezekiah had destroyed.
2. He erected altars for Baal.
3. He made an Asherah (an idol) and put it in the House of the LORD.
4. He worshiped and served the hosts of heaven.
5. He built altars to the hosts of heaven in the two courts of the Temple.
6. He burned his own sons as offerings to the hosts of heaven.
7. He used fortune-telling and omens and dealt with mediums and wizards.
8. He led the people astray to do more evil than any of the pagan nations.
9. He shed much innocent blood.

The LORD spoke to Manasseh and his people, but they paid no attention. Consequently, God promised to destroy Jerusalem. God sent the Assyrian army to capture Manasseh and to take him in chains to Babylon. There Manasseh humbled himself and repented, and he prayed to God. God was moved by Manasseh's prayer. So Manasseh was restored to Jerusalem and his kingdom. Then Manasseh knew that the LORD was God.

When King Manasseh returned to Jerusalem, he was a radically changed person. He built an outer wall for Jerusalem. He strengthened the Army. He then did the following to restore the Mosaic Covenant:

1. He took away the foreign gods, idols, and altars he had placed in the Temple and courts.
2. He restored the altar of the LORD and offered sacrifices to God.
3. He commanded Judah to serve the LORD.

We can learn the following from King Manasseh's life:

1. Sometimes children do exactly the opposite of their pious parents.
2. Even people who become hardened sinners can change to become forgiven saints.
3. Many times people who go through a radical repentance make the best leaders. A good example of this is the apostle Paul.

4. In King Manasseh's radical repentance we can see that others serving Satan can change and become restorers of the New Covenant in our own time.

The good that King Hezekiah had done was destroyed by his son Manasseh. However, when Manasseh came to his senses in that Babylonian dungeon, he was radically changed. When God restored Manasseh to Judah, he tried to restore Judah to God. Yes, Manasseh became a restorer of the Mosaic Covenant after God disciplined and restored him.

King Josiah as a Restorer of the Mosaic Covenant (Reigned 640-604 BC).

We learn about King Josiah in 2 Kings 22:1 to 23:30 and 2 Chronicles 34:1 to 35:23. Josiah was the last good King in Judah, and he was a great example of one seeking restoration of God's will with all his heart. Josiah started his reign when he was just eight years old and reigned over Judah for 31 years. He was complemented by Scripture as doing what was right in the sight of God (2 Kings 22:2; 2 Chronicles 34:2). The following summarizes the life of this great restorer:

1. When King Josiah was 16 years old he began to seek God (2 Chronicles 34:3).
2. When Josiah was 20 years old, he restored the true faith by purging Judah and Jerusalem of the high places and idolatry (2 Chronicles 34:3-7).
3. When Josiah was 26 years old, he restored the house of the LORD (the Temple) (2 Kings 22:3-7; 2 Chronicles 34:8-13).
4. During this restoration of the Temple the lost Book of the Law of Moses was discovered (2 Kings 22:8-13; 2 Chronicles 34:8-21) and it was read aloud to King Josiah. He was immediately shocked and in great sorrow. He had discovered the sins of his people. He had learned that God would bring down His great wrath because of their sins. Faith in God had deteriorated so severely among the people and the priests that losing of the

Book of the Law had not troubled them. In them these Scriptures would be fulfilled:

[6] My people are destroyed for lack of knowledge.
Because you have rejected knowledge,
I also will reject you from being My priest.
Since you have forgotten the law of your God,
I also will forget your children. Hosea 4:6 (NASB)

[13] Therefore My people go into exile for their lack of knowledge;
And their honorable men are famished,
And their multitude is parched with thirst. Isaiah 5:13 (NASB)

5. King Josiah sought the counsel of the LORD. Because Josiah repented and wept, God said the sentence of wrath would come after his death (2 Kings 22:14-20; 2 Chronicles 34:26-28).
6. King Josiah himself read the Book of the Covenant to all the people (2 Kings 23:2; 2 Chronicles 34:29-30).
7. King Josiah made a covenant with the Lord to do his will, and all the people of Judah and Jerusalem joined him and his covenant (2 Kings 23:3; 2 Chronicles 34:31-32).
8. King Josiah removed all the abominations from Israel, and the people were faithful to God during Josiah's lifetime (2 Kings 23:4-25; 2 Chronicles 34:33).
9. When King Josiah was 26 years old, he restored the observance of the Passover (2 Chronicles 35:1, 7-19). He also restored the priesthood and the Levites to their respective roles (2 Kings 23:21-23; 2 Chronicles 35:2-6)
10. This restoration was with a constant eye toward the Book of Moses (2 Chronicles 35:12).
11. Of note is the passage in 2 Chronicles 35:26 where Josiah's deeds of devotion were "according to what is written in the Law of the LORD." Josiah was deeply committed to the Mosaic Covenant and his actions were to restore the Law of the LORD.
12. However, the sinfulness of the Israelite people was too great and even the great efforts of Josiah to restore the Mosaic Covenant

was not enough to avert the wrath of God. Soon after Josiah's death, the people quickly reverted to idolatry and every evil. They were carried away into Babylonian captivity as Huldah had prophesied (2 Kings 22:15-17; 23:26-27; 2 Chronicles 34:23-26; 36:1-21).

The Prophets as Restorers of the Mosaic Covenant

God raised up prophets before the Assyrian Captivity of the Northern 10 tribes in 721 BC, and prophets before the Babylonian Captivity of Judah in 586 BC. Their nearly uniform job assignment was to warn the Jewish kings and the Jewish people that God was going to bring judgment on His chosen people in fulfillment of the Mosaic Covenant.

However, this judgment also came on other countries as well since God is the judge of all peoples. For example, Amos (Amos 1:2 to 2:3) and Jeremiah (Jeremiah chapters 46-51) prophesied punishment to the other Near-Eastern countries. In addition, the reluctant prophet Jonah was sent with the message of judgment to Assyria.

God again raised up additional prophets for the special needs of His chosen people when they returned from Babylonian Captivity. Significant encouragement was required for the Jewish people who had become slaves of the Persian Kings. The discouragement from their pagan neighbors was very great, and this significantly delayed the rebuilding of the Temple, which was the primary charge from the Persian King Cyrus (Isaiah 44:28; 45:1-13; 2 Chronicles 36:22-24; Ezra 1:2-4).

Just as has been illustrated thus far, we have established beyond reasonable doubt that there were restorers of the Mosaic Covenant beginning with Moses and continuing through Joshua, the Judges, and some of the Judean kings. Now we should acknowledge that the prophets also played a critical role in the never-ceasing job of restoring the Mosaic Covenant in Old Testament times.

The volume of the prophetic writings in the Old Testament is very large, most especially the Major Prophets. However, we can be assured that the prophets did not come with some kind of new religion. Rather, their assignment was to bring the people back to the Mosaic Covenant. Their great difficulty was that the people tended to be "corrupt" from the time of the Judges even through the end of the Southern Kingdom (Judges 2:19; 2 Chronicles 27:2). There had been a few windows of enlightenment, restoration, and obedience for the Southern Kingdom; however, most of this period was spent without regard to God's law.

The word "law" is used in 30 verses in the Major Prophets (Isaiah through Daniel). Some of these scriptures prophetically speak of a future law (Isaiah 2:3; 42:4; 51:4; Jeremiah 31:31-33). However, most speak of the existing Mosaic Covenant/Law. In this regard, the word "law" is often described as belonging to God with such terms as "the LORD's Law," "My Law," "God's Law," "His Law," or "the Law of Moses" (Isaiah 5:24; 42:21, 24; 51:4, 7; Jeremiah 2:8; 6:19; 8:8; 9:13; 16:11; 26:4; 32:23; 44:10, 23; Lamentations 2:9; Ezekiel 7:26; 22:26; 43:12; Daniel 6:5; 7:25; 9:11, 13).

The word "law" in the Minor Prophets (Hosea-Malachi) occurs in nine verses and is similarly translated "Law of God," "My Covenant," "My Law," "Law of the LORD," and "Law of my servant Moses that I commanded him" (Hosea 4:6; 8:1; Amos 2:4; Habakkuk 1:4; Zephaniah 3:4; Zechariah 7:12; Malachi 4:4). It is also used for future law in Micah 4:2. It should be noted that nearly the last verse of prophecy in the Old Testament resounded this note of restoration:

> [4] "Remember the law of Moses My servant, even the statutes and ordinances which I commanded him in Horeb for all Israel. Malachi 4:4 (NASB)

Therefore, it is very clear that the customary term "law" among the prophets clearly was understood as the Mosaic Law. The prophets did not invent a new religion with a new law. Rather, they tried with all the words they could speak and write to bring the people out of sin and back to the Covenant God had made with Moses and the Israelites. There was no other standard.

This is important. If the Law was given to Moses in about 1446 BC, and if Malachi wrote as the last Old Testament prophet in about 445 BC, then God had not changed his mind about this matter of Covenant for about 1000 years. Regardless of the massive changes in culture, regardless of the constant pressure of the pagan religions, and regardless of some who viewed the Mosaic Covenant as being obsolete, God had not changed His mind. At the end of the Old Testament, God was still judging them by the Mosaic Law that was 1000 years old.

Yet, the Mosaic Law was valid even longer than 1000 years. Christ was born under the Mosaic Law (Galatians 4:4). Christ sealed with His own blood (Hebrews 9:12) the New Covenant (Luke 22:20; 1 Corinthians 11:25; 2 Corinthians 3:6; Hebrews 9:15; 12:24). Thus, God maintained the Mosaic Covenant/Law about 1500 years until the crucifixion of Christ.

In summary, the prophets were definitely restorers of the Mosaic Covenant/Law. They didn't make up their own religion based upon the whims of the Jewish people or the Jewish kings. Rather, they were faithful to the God of the Mosaic Covenant.

Therefore, let us be faithful to the God of the New Covenant. Let us never grow weary in restoring that New Covenant in all the churches of Christ. Let us be as Paul exhorted the Corinthians:

> [58] Therefore, my beloved brethren, be steadfast, immovable, always abounding in the work of the Lord, knowing that your toil is not in vain in the Lord. 1 Corinthians 15:58 (NASB)

Study Questions

1. Several of the kings repeatedly tried to make treaties and covenants with other nations (including covenants between Judah and Israel). Was this pleasing to God? (2 Chronicles 19:1-3; 2 Corinthians 6:14-18)
2. Is it good for a Christian to seek care from physicians and not ask God for help as King Asa did? (2 Chronicles 16:12; James 5:13-15)
3. Was King Jehoshaphat evangelistic in the public reading of the Book of the Law and in calling the people back to God?
4. If our faith is dependent on the faith of someone else, what will happen to our faith when that other person is gone?
5. What happened when King Uzziah became proud and went into the Temple to burn incense? Does this teach us the principle that

we must worship only according to God's commands and not the teachings of men?

6. How can you personally order your ways according to the Lord your God as King Jotham did?
7. A bad king, King Ahaz, had a son, the good King Hezekiah, who was deeply committed to God. Is a vibrant faith inherited or is it a personal choice?
8. The good King Hezekiah had a son, the evil King Manasseh. Did the evil King Manasseh undo all the good his father King Hezekiah did? Did the evil King Manasseh repent in prison in Babylon? Did God restore King Manasseh to his throne? Did King Manasseh then try hard to do only what was right in the sight of God?
9. King Josiah was the last good king in Judah. What did he do when they read the lost Book of the Covenant to him? Did King Josiah personally read the lost Book of the Covenant to the people?
10. Did the prophets preach a new doctrine, or did they draw the people back to the Mosaic Covenant?

Chapter 4

Mosaic Covenant: Daniel to the Maccabees

Daniel and His Friends as Restorers of the Mosaic Covenant (606-536 BC)

Daniel was a prophet ministering to the Babylonian and Medo-Persian kings from 605 through at least 539 BC. He was exiled to Babylon in 605 BC as a young man, and was indoctrinated into the literature and language of the Chaldeans. The training was designed to convert Daniel and the other young Jewish men to be like the pagan Chaldeans rather than the God-worshiping Jews.

The Temple and the Temple worship were gone—both had been destroyed by the Babylonians. Daniel could have easily become a Chaldean and that would have saved him from a lot of trials. However, Daniel refused to become an idol worshiper. He refused to turn his back on the LORD and His Law. In the midst of this horde of pagans, Daniel conducted himself so that the LORD would be glorified. Christians have much to learn from the personal example of Daniel.

All three issues that follow have something to do with idolatry, which was forbidden in the Mosaic Law (Exodus 20:1-6). First there was the matter of the food the King provided to Daniel and his friends (Daniel 1). Undoubtedly, the food was offered to an idol before being dispensed to Daniel and his friends for their consumption. In addition, the Chaldeans did not observe the food restrictions of the Hebrews under the Mosaic Law. As a result, Daniel and his three friends would have been defiled if they had eaten the King's food (Leviticus 11:47; Ezekiel 4:13-14; Hosea 9:3). So they pleaded with the chief of the eunuchs that they be allowed to eat vegetables and water instead of the King's food and wine. The LORD blessed them for making this choice for Him.

Second, there was the matter of the King's forced idol worship (Daniel 3). The Babylonian King Nebuchadnezzar made a huge idol of gold and commanded all people to fall down and worship that idol. However, Daniel's three friends refused to do this as it would be idolatry (Exodus 20:1-6). The King threatened them, and when they would not change their minds, he had them thrown into the fiery furnace. But God blessed them and protected them from the fire.

Third, there was the issue of forced praying to the King instead of praying to God (Daniel 6). This was also a form of idolatry. It was a plot by several pagan officials to remove Daniel from his chief position in the government. Darius the Mead had set up this government after Cyrus conquered Babylon. The pagan officials could find no accusation against Daniel unless they found it "...in regard to the law of his God" (Daniel 6:5). Daniel continued to pray three times a day to God, just as he had always done, and so these evil pagan officials were able to accuse Daniel before Darius the King.

Although Darius tried to deliver Daniel from the Law of the Medes and Persians, he could not. Therefore, he commanded that Daniel be thrown into a den of lions, but before it was done, Darius said to Daniel, "May your God, whom you serve continually, deliver you!" (Daniel 6:16 ESV). God shut the mouths of lions, and they did no harm to Daniel, so Daniel was saved by God because of his love and obedience to God. Daniel, like his three friends, would rather die than go against the command of God in the Mosaic Law.

Therefore, Daniel and his three friends were restorers of the Mosaic Law while they lived among the pagans. Because of this, the pagans learned that there is a God in Heaven, the one, true and living God. Furthermore, Daniel and his three friends, by their standing for God in the midst of the outcry to abandon God, showed an eternal principle for all people. This is the same eternal principle Peter declared: "We must obey God rather than men" (Acts 5:29 NASB).

Whether we are faced with the idol of materialism in the West or the idols found in Africa, India, or the Orient, we must turn our backs on these forms of idolatry and serve God instead. Daniel and friends chose to restore the Mosaic Covenant. In like manner, now we must restore the New Covenant by obeying and serving God rather than men.

Jeshua & Zerubbabel as Restorers of the Mosaic Covenant (536-515 BC)

In 536 BC the Persian king Cyrus released the first Jewish captives so that they could return to Jerusalem and Judea under Zerubbabel and Jeshua. They went with the primary charge from Cyrus to rebuild the Temple of God in Jerusalem and to offer sacrifices to God (2 Chronicles 36:23; Ezra 1:2-4).

After the Jews arrived from their long journey, Jeshua and his fellow priests and Zerubbabel promptly rebuilt the Altar to the LORD "...as it was written in the Law of Moses the man of God" (Ezra 3:2 NASB). They also restored the Feast of Booths (Ezra 3:4) at that time. Therefore, it is clear that these Jews had a heart to restore the Mosaic Covenant.

The rebuilding of the Temple, which was the primary charge of King Cyrus, was started in the second year of their return by Jeshua and Zerubbabel. However, because of the opposition from their pagan neighbors and a subsequent decree from the Persian King Artaxeres, the work ceased for many years (Ezra 4). Therefore, God raised up the prophets Haggai and Zechariah and this in turn gave strength to Zerubbabel and Jeshua to finish the Temple in 515 BC.

There was continuing opposition from their pagan neighbors. When the opposition sent their complaints to King Darius, he ordered that a search be made of the archives. They found the decree of King Cyrus regarding this issue (Ezra 6). Consequently, King Darius ordered the officials to help the Jews rebuilt the Temple by providing raw materials and finances.

It should be noted that after the Temple was dedicated, they restored the roles of the priests and Levites in the Temple "... as it is written in the book of Moses" (Ezra 6:18 NASB). They also restored the observances of both the Passover and the Feast of Unleavened Bread (Ezra 6:19-22).

Therefore, it should be clear that these Jews had hearts which sought the restoration of the Mosaic Covenant, which they saw as God's Law. In this respect, they were very different from their fathers in the days of the prophet Jeremiah. Jeremiah tried so hard for so long and suffered so much persecution, but those Jews would not do what God commanded:

> [16] Thus says the LORD,
> "Stand by the ways and see and ask for the ancient paths,
> Where the good way is, and walk in it;
> And you shall find rest for your souls.
> But they said, 'We will not walk in it.'" Jeremiah 6:16 (NASB)
> (see also Isaiah 8:20; Malachi 4:4)

It is tragic to see the stubbornness of the Jews, especially knowing that they would be decimated and taken into captivity because of it.

From this we must recognize that, in those ancient times, God did not approve nor recognize any teachings of men that were contrary to His Covenant with Moses. This should stand as a stark warning to us. Man always wants something new, something to tickle his fancies. Unfortunately, many of the practices of so-called "Christianity" of today bear no resemblance to what was shown and commanded in the New Covenant. When these self-willed people are asked to return to the New Testament as God's authority in worship and church government, yes, even seeking the "ancient paths" of Christianity, they also respond like the Jews in Jeremiah 6:16, saying, "We will not walk in it."

God's position regarding His word to Moses was very clear:

> [2] "You shall not add to the word which I am commanding you, nor take away from it, that you may keep the commandments of the LORD your God which I command you." Deuteronomy 4:2 (NASB)

> [32] "Whatever I command you, you shall be careful to do; you shall not add to nor take away from it." Deuteronomy 12:32 (NASB)

Later, the following confirmation of this concept was written:

> [6] Do not add to His words
> Lest He reprove you, and you be proved a liar. Proverbs 30:6 (NASB)

However, these warnings to not add and to not take away from God's Word are not confined to the Mosaic Covenant. These warnings are repeated at the very end of the New Covenant:

> [18] I testify to everyone who hears the words of the prophecy of this book: if anyone adds to them, God shall add to him the plagues which are written in this book; [19] and if anyone takes away from the words of the book of this prophecy, God shall take away his part from the tree of life and from the holy city, which are written in this book. Revelation 22:18-19 (NASB)

We too must be very concerned about this cardinal principle of understanding Scripture; that is, to know what was written by God's inspiration, and not to go beyond what has been written (1 Corinthians 4:6). If we say we will follow Christ's words, we also must follow the words of his apostles (John 15:20). This is because Christ promised that He would send the Holy Spirit on the apostles, and the Holy Spirit would guide the apostles into all truth (John 16:13). We must live by every word that comes from the mouth of God (Matthew 4:4) and that includes the New Covenant because God's word is truth (John 17:17). We must never allow the traditions of man to make void the Word of God (Matthew 15:6; Mark 7:13). We must not only hear the Word of God, but we must also keep it (Luke 11:28). If we don't keep the Words of Jesus, His Word will judge us in the last day (John 12:48). If we love Jesus, we will keep His Word (John 14:23). If we don't obey Jesus' Word, we do not love Him (John 14:24).

Christians, I must ask you: Do you really think God will be pleased if we add to or take away from His commands in the New Covenant? Can we ignore such fundamental principles concerning how we handle God's Word and still be pleasing to him?

Ezra as a Restorer of the Mosaic Covenant (458 BC)

In 458 BC, Ezra the scribe/priest requested that Persian King Artaxerxes send him back to Jerusalem (Ezra 7:1-6). King Artaxerxes did so, and put his charge to Ezra as stated in Ezra 7:12-26. Ezra was "... learned in matters of the commandments of the LORD and his statutes for Israel..." (Ezra 7:11 ESV). Specifically, Ezra was to "... make inquiries about Judah and Jerusalem according to the Law of your God, which is in your hand..." (Ezra 7:14 ESV). Ezra was to bear many gifts from King Artaxerxes to the House of God in Jerusalem (Ezra 7:15-20). Ezra also was charged to do the following:

> 23 "Whatever is commanded by the God of heaven, let it be done with zeal for the house of the God of heaven, lest there be wrath against the kingdom of the king and his sons." Ezra 7:23 (NASB)

In addition, Ezra was to judge all the Jews and teach those who did not know the Law. Ezra was also charged to administer punishment on anyone who refused to obey God's Law or the King's Law (Ezra 7:25-26).

When Ezra arrived in Jerusalem, he immediately restored God's Law of Marriage for the Jews (Exodus 34:11-16; Deuteronomy 7:1-4) because there were many who had foreign wives (Ezra 9:1 to 10:44). In addition, Ezra read from the Law to all the people, and certain Levites helped the people understand the Law (Nehemiah 8:1-8). The people wept when they heard the law.

The Feast of Booths was also celebrated (Nehemiah 8:13-18) according to the "Law that the LORD had commanded by Moses..." (Nehemiah 8:14 ESV). The people "...came together to Ezra the scribe in order to study the words of the Law" (Nehemiah 8:13 ESV). Ezra read to the people every day of the feast from the Book of the Law of God.

The people understood their sins and assembled themselves while wearing sackcloth and ashes (Nehemiah 9:1). They confessed their sins, and they read from the Book of the Law of the LORD. They prayed to God and made a covenant (Nehemiah 9:6-38). This covenant was a curse and an oath to walk in God's Law and to observe all the Commandments of the LORD. They said they would obey God's command regarding marriage, would observe the Sabbath, would give the annual third part of the shekel for the house of the LORD, would give all other offerings, and would observe all other feast days and all other obligations. In a word, they obligated themselves to obey the whole Law of Moses (Nehemiah 10:28-39).

Thus, Ezra was able to bring all the Jews into an awakening and a restoration of the Law of Moses. He approached this in such a way that all the people participated and gave full allegiance to God's Law. The repeated readings of the Book of the Law of God were a vital key to this revival and restoration. Ezra was faithful in all matters before God and the Persian King Artaxerxes. Ezra was a restorer of God's Law to Moses and a wonderful teacher of the Law of God.

We should pray for such a revival and restoration today. Many people who call themselves Christians today know very little about the Bible. May God give us the strength and willingness to restore His New Covenant. May God cause us to open our Bibles again and to read afresh the New Testament that we may weep because of our sins and rejoice because of God's salvation.

Christians, it is time for us to restore the New Covenant.

Nehemiah as a Restorer of the Mosaic Covenant (445 BC)

Thirteen years after Ezra came to Jerusalem, Nehemiah made a similar journey in 445 BC. This was 91 years after Cyrus released the Jews to return to Jerusalem. Nehemiah had heard from travelers that Jerusalem had serious troubles. He was the cupbearer to the Persian King Artaxerxes. In the 20th year of the King's reign, Nehemiah asked to be sent to Judah so that he might rebuild the city of Jerusalem. The major issue was that the walls and gates had not been rebuilt.

Nehemiah is best known for leading the people of Jerusalem to rebuild the city's walls and gates. Of course, this great effort did not restore the Mosaic Covenant, but it did cause great joy for all the Jews. However, Nehemiah was instrumental in the following reforms which definitely were restorations of the Mosaic Covenant:

1. He stopped the rich Jews from exacting interest from the poor Jews (Nehemiah 5:1-13; Exodus 22:25; Leviticus 25:36; Psalms 15:5; Ezekiel 22:12).
2. He restored the service at the Temple and specifically the service of the priests, Levites, singers and gatekeepers. He made sure that these were properly supported by the Jews (Nehemiah 12:44-47; 13:10-14).
3. Again, the reading of the Law for all people was accomplished (Nehemiah 13:1; Exodus 24:7; Deuteronomy 31:10-11).
4. Nehemiah separated all those of foreign descent from Israel (Nehemiah 13:30; Deuteronomy 23:3-6).
5. He restored the observance of the Sabbath and especially kept it holy (Nehemiah 13:15-22; Exodus 20:8-10).
6. A recurrent problem of Jews marrying foreign wives was confronted (Nehemiah 13:23-29; Exodus 34:11-16; Deuteronomy 7:1-4).

All of Nehemiah's actions in these areas constituted continual efforts to restore the Mosaic Law among the Jews. We too must never give up restoring the New Covenant today.

The examples of Ezra and Nehemiah are of special significance to us today. These men were servants of God and they knew the written Word of God. However, they were without any evidence of a special divine call or prophetic appointment from God. Rather, they were convicted by the written Word of God, they lived by the Word of God, and they taught the Word of God. Brothers and sisters in Christ, we can do that today. Are you willing to imitate Ezra or Nehemiah today so that people will know and obey the New Covenant?

The Persian Kings, Cyrus and Artaxerxes, as Restorers of the Mosaic Covenant

It should not come as any surprise that God used pagan kings who did not know Him to accomplish His own divine will. For example, God clearly used Pharaoh to accomplish His purpose of freeing the Israelites from Egyptian captivity and leading them to safety. Nevertheless, we certainly cannot say that Pharaoh was willing to be God's servant because he truly struggled against God's will. But his struggle was to no avail and only resulted in his own demise in the Red Sea (Psalm 136:15).

However, when we come to the Persian King Cyrus, even Isaiah prophesied concerning him long before Cyrus was born (Isaiah 44:28; 45:1). God called Cyrus, who had not yet been born, His servant. God says concerning Cyrus,

> 4 "For the sake of Jacob My servant,
> And Israel My chosen one,
> I have also called you by your name;
> I have given you a title of honor
> Though you have not known Me." Isaiah 45:4 (NASB)

As we have seen, "... the LORD stirred up the spirit of Cyrus king of Persia..." to make a proclamation that allowed the Jews to return to Jerusalem and rebuild the Temple/House of the LORD (Ezra 1:1-4). Cyrus himself clearly said that "The LORD, the God of heaven...has charged me to build him a house at Jerusalem..." (Ezra 1:2 ESV).

Perhaps Cyrus became aware of Isaiah's prophecy concerning him; yet, this would not account for God's specific charge to rebuild the Temple. Perhaps God spoke to Cyrus in a dream or a vision. Certainly God spoke to the Gentile prophet Balaam in this manner (Numbers chapters 22 to 24), so we should not exclude that possibility with Cyrus.

However, notice that it is God who is initiating this action by Cyrus. Therefore, the inescapable conclusion concerning Cyrus is that this Persian King was an instrument of God to restore the Mosaic Covenant, for that is what the Temple symbolized. This action by Cyrus restored Temple worship to God which was the foundation for Jewish faith.

The Persian King Artaxerxes sent Ezra the priest/scribe with the specific charge to restore the Mosaic Law among the Jews (Ezra 7:14, 25-26). Artaxerxes addressed his charge "...to Ezra the priest, the scribe of the Law of the God of heaven" (Ezra 7:12 ESV). Ezra's restoration of the Mosaic Law went deeper than just the Temple worship. This restoration touched multiple aspects of daily Jewish life, including illegal marriages to foreigners (Ezra, chapters 9 to 10), as well as other issues such as violations of the Sabbath Law, offerings, new moons, appointed feasts, holy things, first fruits, and tithes (Nehemiah 10:28-39).

Thus, we see that these two pagan Persian Kings commanded restoration of the Mosaic Law among the Jews. Cyrus explicitly attributes this to the God of heaven. Artaxerxes commanded these restorations because of the God of heaven "...lest His wrath be against the realm of the king and his sons" (Ezra 7:23 ESV).

These were restorations brought about by the will and actions of God Almighty through pagan kings. Praise God, for it is He who caused every restoration of the Mosaic Covenant from Moses, Joshua, the Judges, David, the Judean kings, the prophets, pagan Persian Kings, as well as Ezra and Nehemiah. Our God has shown His love for Covenant Restoration by His relentless, persistent and repetitive actions over 1000 years of biblical history. Praises to the God of Covenant relationship! Let us give glory to the God of restoration, yes, restoration of even His New Covenant.

The Maccabees as Restorers of the Mosaic Covenant (175-63 BC)

The Old Testament ends with the writings of the prophet Malachi. Thus, there were about 400 years of prophetic silence from the close of Malachi until the birth of Christ. During these 400 years of prophetic silence, there were many non-canonical books written, and some of these contain accurate historical information, though they are not considered inspired by God. These historical accounts are very helpful in our understanding about what happened to God's chosen people during those 400 years of prophetic silence.

It should be noted, however, that the magnificent prophecies God gave to Daniel in the sixth century BC included prophecies about this period of prophetic silence from 400 BC to the birth of Christ. God revealed to Daniel the coming of five great kingdoms:

1. Babylonian (Daniel 2:36-38; 7:4)—Babylon fell to Cyrus and 538 BC.

2. Medes and Persians (Daniel 2:39; 5:28-31; 7:5; 10:20; 11:2)—Darius the Mede was defeated in 333 BC by Alexander the Great.
3. Greece (Daniel 2:39; 7:6; 8:5-14, 21-26; 10:20)—Rome defeated Greece in a series of military conflicts.
4. Rome (Daniel 2:40-43; 7:7-8, 19-25)—Rome defeated Israel in 63 BC. (Constantine established Constantinople as capital of the Roman Empire in AD 330. The Roman Empire was divided into Eastern and Western Empires in AD 395. The Western Empire fragmented. Rome was sacked in AD 410. In 476 the rule of Rome in the West came to an end. The fall of remnants of the Eastern Roman Empire occurred when they were absorbed into the Ottoman Empire in AD 1453.)
5. An Everlasting World-Wide Kingdom (Daniel 2:44-45; 7:13-14, 17, 18, 27)—this is Christ's Kingdom, established in AD 30 during the time of Roman rule.

Therefore, during most of these 400 years of prophetic silence, Greece was the ruling world kingdom. Josephus records that Jerusalem welcomed Alexander the Great, and the High Priest showed Alexander the prophecy of Daniel (Daniel 8:1-8, 20-21) that Alexander would defeat the kings of Media and Persia (Josephus). Because of this, Alexander the Great allowed the Jews to live according to their own laws and without the obligation to pay taxes to Greece. This was in 332 BC.

However, with Alexander's early death in 323 BC, and as prophesied by Daniel 8:22, Alexander's kingdom was divided among his four generals. Also as prophesied in Daniel 11:5-45, there were multiple conflicts between the Northern (Seleucids) kingdom and the Southern (Ptolemies) kingdom. Unfortunately, Israel was geographically between these two kingdoms, so Israel suffered much because of the hostilities.

The greatest challenge to the Jewish faith under Greek rule was Alexander's plan to "Hellenize" all of his kingdom. This meant all the countries he conquered were to learn the Greek language, culture, and religion. These nations were urged to adopt the Grecian way of life. Unfortunately, the Grecian culture was based on polytheism and idolatry. This brought about every kind of sexual immorality and drunkenness, and these were manifested throughout the Grecian Empire.

The Jews were under the Ptolemies from 323-198 BC, and they generally did well. During this period the Septuagint (LXX), or the Greek translation of the Old Testament, was produced. It became the Scriptures for all the Jews throughout the empire except for the Jews in Jerusalem who continued to use the Hebrew translation.

From 198-166 BC, Israel came under the control and rule of the Seleucids. In 175 BC, Antiochus IV Epiphanes came to power over the Seleucid kingdom. The non-canonical history books of first and second Maccabees tell us about this horrible time when Antiochus forced Jews to renounce the Mosaic Law and to live like Greeks instead of Jews. Any Jew who refused was sentenced to torture and murder. Antiochus IV Epiphanes made circumcision a capital offense for the baby, the mother, the family, and the one who performed the circumcision. He stole all the riches of the Temple, and he desecrated the Altar and the Temple by sacrificing a pig on the altar to his own pagan god.

When the forces of Antiochus tried to force a priest named Mattathias to abandon his faith, Mattathias rebelled and killed many Greek soldiers. His family then retreated to the hill country. After his death, his son Judas Maccabees organized men to fight against Antiochus. These men loved God and the Law of Moses. Judas regained Jerusalem, built a new Altar, restored the Temple, rededicated it, restored the daily sacrifices, and initiated a special feast called "Hanukkah" which celebrated this event.

Over the following years, all of Mattathias' sons and two grandsons lost their lives in the fight for the true God and the Mosaic Law. However, what they accomplished was an independent Israel that could worship according to God's Law. This led to the dynasty of Hasmonean Priests and lasted until the Romans took over Israel in 63 BC.

The Maccabees, as they were called, were brave, determined, and zealous Jewish believers in God. They attributed all their successes to God, and they prayed to Him in all situations. This history is not found in the Protestant Bible, just as we don't find our own history in the Bible. However, we find in first and second Maccabees people who loved God and gave Him their all so that they could worship according to God's Law. The Maccabees were restorers of the Mosaic Law.

Do we have such brave, determined, and zealous Christians today who will restore the New Covenant?

Study Questions

1. How did Daniel and his friends restore the Mosaic Covenant while they were slaves in pagan Babylon? What implications does this have for us today?
2. How did Jeshua, his fellow priests, and Zerubbabel restore the Mosaic Covenant when they returned as slaves to Palestine from Babylonian captivity?
3. A large part of Ezra's ministry was reading the Law to the people. Did this cause an awakening and a restoration of the Mosaic Covenant?
4. Is there any evidence that either Ezra or Nehemiah had a divine call or appointment for their ministries? How do we compare to them today?
5. Explain how God used the pagan Persian Kings Cyrus and Artaxerxes to rebuild the Temple and restore the Mosaic Covenant to the Jews.
6. Explain how the Maccabees were restorers of the Mosaic Covenant in the second century BC.

Chapter 5

God's Covenant with David (1010-970 BC)

Many say this covenant God made with David was Unilateral—that is, it required nothing from David. This covenant was given by God when David purposed to build a house for God in about 1000 B.C. Indeed, it appears to be Unilateral at the beginning. The following characterizes this covenant:

1. Prologue (2 Samuel 7:4-7)
2. Promises/Blessings (2 Samuel 7:8-16)
   a. David chosen by God (vs 8)
   b. God to cut off all David's enemies (vs 9)
   c. God to make David's name great (vs 9)
   d. God to bless Israel (vs 10-11)
   e. God to give David rest from his enemies (vs 11)
   f. God to establish the kingdom with David's offspring (vs 11-12)
   g. God to discipline David's offspring, but will continue to show steadfast love to them (vs 14-15)

The implied ***conditional nature*** of God's blessings became clear to David when he committed adultery with Bathsheba and then murdered her husband, Uriah (2 Samuel 11). Then it was announced to David by

Nathan the prophet (2 Samuel 12). The following were the judgments of God against David, and these would erode the blessings God had promised:

1. The sword would never depart from David's house.
2. God raised up evil against David out of David's house.
3. Bathsheba's child died.

In addition, the ***conditional nature*** of God's blessings on the linage of kings who came from David also became very clear to David. Although David realized that God had made an "everlasting covenant" with him (2 Samuel 23:5), David exhorted Solomon to faithfulness, and quoted God as saying, "If your sons…" (1 Kings 2:4), which portrayed the language of conditional blessings for the future Davidic kings. This same conditional nature was shown in 1 Chronicles 22:13; 28:7-9; 2 Chronicles 6:16; 7:17-22; and Psalms 132:11-12, "If your sons keep…."

David's exhortation to Solomon was not in vain because Solomon understood the conditional nature of God's blessings (2 Chronicles 6:16). However, Solomon had an unfortunate gap between understanding God and obeying God. Solomon violated God's special covenant with him in multiple ways. For example, Solomon multiplied horses, multiplied silver and gold (1 Kings 10:14-29), multiplied wives and concubines (1 Kings 11:1-3), built Temples for his foreign wives' gods, and Solomon worshipped those false gods (1 Kings 11:4-8). All these were against God's Law (Exodus 20:3-6; Deuteronomy 17:16-17). Because of Solomon's unfaithfulness, the house of David lost the 10 Northern tribes in 930 B.C. (1 Kings 11:29-39). Because of the continued unfaithfulness of most of Judean kings over the next three centuries, Judah and all the house of David went into Babylonian captivity in 606-586 BC. This ended the earthly reign of the house of David.

Therefore, one should not view God's covenant with David as Unilateral on the part of God. Implicit in this covenant was an expectation that David must continue to follow the Law of Moses. David deserved death according to the Mosaic Law because of his adultery with Bathsheba and his murder of Uriah, her husband. God showed extreme grace and mercy when He did not utterly destroy David. God, in spite of the ungodly behavior of most of the Judean Kings, bore with that situation on behalf of His covenant with David, that there might be a "lamp" for David (1 Kings 11:36; 15:4; 2 Kings 8:19; 2 Chronicles 21:7). However, from 568 B.C. to the present, there has been no earthly ruler of Israel who came from the house of David.

Therefore, the only thing that remains, and will remain into eternity, is that David's throne will stand eternally before God. This was, and is, and will continue to be fulfilled in Jesus Christ (Luke 1:32-33, 69; Acts 2:30-31; Revelation 3:7). This was the spiritual fulfillment of God's promise since the earthly rule of the house of David came to an end in 586 B.C.

Restorations of God's Covenant with David

God's Preservation of the Earthly House of David

God established His covenant with David during the reign of David 1010-970 BC. God renewed that covenant with Solomon (970-930 BC). Because of the extreme unfaithfulness of Solomon to the Mosaic Covenant, the monarchy of Israel was dissolved, and the house of David was left with only two of the 12 tribes.

The northern 10 tribes were led by Jeroboam I, and he established idolatry from the very beginning of his reign. Nineteen more Israelite kings reigned over the northern 10 tribes. Total reigns of the kings of Israel were from 932-721 BC. There were no good kings who followed God in the northern kingdom. Samaria, the capital of the northern kingdom, fell in 721 BC, and all of the northern 10 tribes went into Assyrian captivity.

However, God preserved the southern kingdom of Judah with its two tribes from 930 to 586 BC. As we have previously identified, there were eight good kings in Judah, and this appears to be the reason why the southern kingdom lasted 135 years longer than the northern kingdom. It should be noted that after Solomon, there were 20 kings who ruled in the northern kingdom, and there were also 20 kings who ruled in the southern kingdom. The substantially longer survival of the southern kingdom with the same number of kings as the northern kingdom certainly shows God's preservation of the house of David.

In total, the house of David stood for approximately 420 years. Jerusalem was then destroyed in 586 BC. All the people in the southern kingdom were taken into Babylonian captivity, and this ended the earthly reign of the house of David.

God's Revival of the House of David in His Offspring, Jesus Christ

The future revival of the House of David was announced by the prophet Amos between 760-750 BC:

> [11] "In that day I will raise up the fallen booth of David,
> And wall up its breaches;
> I will also raise up its ruins
> And rebuild it as in the days of old;
> [12] That they may possess the remnant of Edom
> And all the nations who are called by My name,"
> Declares the LORD who does this. Amos 9:11-12 (NASB)

James quotes this passage (Acts 15:16-17) as evidence that the Gentiles would also be granted entry into the church. However, for our purposes here, this passage is speaking of the revival of the House of David in the first century AD.

This revival of the House of David in the first century AD was centered in the coming of Jesus Christ. He was in the linage of David and therefore called the Son of David (Matthew 1:1, 6, 17, 20; 9:27; 12:23; 15:22; 20:30-31; 21:9, 15; Mark 10:47-48; 11:10; Luke 1:27, 32, 69; 2:4, 11; 3:31; 18:38-39; John 7:42; Acts 2:34; Romans 1:3; 2 Timothy 2:8; Revelation 5:5; 22:16). Luke clearly states that Christ came to possess the throne of David and to reign over the house of Jacob forever:

> [31] "And behold, you will conceive in your womb, and bear a son,
> and you shall name Him Jesus. [32] He will be great, and will be
> called the Son of the Most High; and the Lord God will give Him

the throne of His father David; [33] and He will reign over the house of Jacob forever; and His kingdom will have no end." Luke 1:31-33 (NASB)

In retrospect, then, we can understand God's promise to David; that it could not be confined to just an earthly kingdom of Jews, but an eternal kingdom of all people "...who are called by My name." This is what Christ is now reigning over from heaven, and it is an eternal kingdom.

Christ knew that He would not be the earthly ruler of the Jews, and that His Kingdom was not of this world:

> [33] Therefore Pilate entered again into the Praetorium, and summoned Jesus and said to Him, "Are You the King of the Jews?"
> [34] Jesus answered, "Are you saying this on your own initiative, or did others tell you about Me?" [35] Pilate answered, "I am not a Jew, am I? Your own nation and the chief priests delivered You to me; what have You done?" [36] Jesus answered, "My kingdom is not of this world. If My kingdom were of this world, then My servants would be fighting so that I would not be handed over to the Jews; but as it is, My kingdom is not of this realm." [37] Therefore Pilate said to Him, "So You are a king?" Jesus answered, "You say correctly that I am a king. For this I have been born, and for this I have come into the world, to testify to the truth. Everyone who is of the truth hears My voice." [38] Pilate said to Him, "What is truth?" John 18:33-38 (NASB)

After Christ's resurrection from the dead and His ascension, Scripture consistently speaks of Him being at the right hand of God (Mark 16:19; Acts 2:33; 7:55-56; Romans 8:34; Colossians 3:1; Hebrews 10:12; 1 Peter 3:22).

Therefore, we find that God fulfilled His covenant with David by the sending of His own Son, who was born in the linage of King David, who was proclaimed to be the son of David, and who now reigns forever on the eternal and heavenly throne of David. God restored His Covenant with David after it ceased to be an earthly throne in 586 BC. He restored His Covenant with David half a millennium later with the coming of His own Son.

Study Questions

1. Was the covenant God made with David without stated conditions? (2 Samuel 7:4-15)
2. David committed adultery with Bathsheba and had her husband, Uriah, murdered. God then reversed some of the covenant promises He had made to David (2 Samuel 12). Is this fair on God's part since this was a special covenant with David and his linage?
3. Was David still under the Law of Moses when he did these evil things, or did God's special covenant with David make the Law of Moses null and void for David?
4. What was the penalty for murder in God's Covenant with Noah? (Genesis 9:5-6) What was the penalty for murder in the Mosaic Covenant? (Exodus 21:12) What was the penalty for adultery in the Mosaic Covenant? (Leviticus 20:10) What penalty did David deserve? Did God treat David with grace and mercy, or did He treat him according to what David deserved?
5. Is it fair to say that in all covenants God has made with men, these covenants are indeed conditional when it comes to men's behaviors?
6. Is it fair to say that the most basic and pervasive expectations God has of man in any covenant relationship is that man must have a trusting faith in God and must obey what God commands? (For example, consider the hymn, *Trust and Obey*)
7. Regarding the throne promise to David, it was conditional also. Jerusalem fell in 586 BC. Since that time there has never been an earthly king after the linage of David sitting on David's throne in Jerusalem. So how is the throne promise to David fulfilled now?

Chapter 6

God's New Covenant with Jesus Christ

God's New Covenant with His Son

God's New Covenant was prophesied in the Old Testament in the following verses: Isaiah 42:6; 49:8; 55:3; 59:21; 61:8; Jeremiah 31:31-34; 32:40; 50:5; Ezekiel 16:60-63; 20:37; 34:25; 37:26-28; Hosea 2:18. ***Christ is the New Covenant*** (Isaiah 42:6-7; 49:8). This New Covenant is contained within the New Testament. The following summarizes the New Covenant:

1. Preamble—Old Testament Messianic Prophecies
2. Historical Prologue—The Gospels: Matthew, Mark, Luke and John, that is, the life of Christ.
3. Invitation to Enter the Covenant—Matthew 11:28-30

    28 "Come to Me, all who are weary and heavy-laden, and I will give you rest. 29 Take My yoke upon you, and learn from Me, for I am gentle and humble in heart; and YOU SHALL FIND REST FOR YOUR SOULS. 30 For My yoke is easy, and My load is light." Matt 11:28-30 (NASB)

4. The Terms of the Covenant—obeying Christ and His apostles.

Obedience to Christ is of upmost importance for the Christian:

[36] "He who believes in the Son has eternal life; but he who does not obey the Son shall not see life, but the wrath of God abides on him." John 3:36 (NASB)

[51] "Truly, truly, I say to you, if anyone keeps My word he shall never see death." John 8:51 (NASB)

[20] "teaching them to observe all that I commanded you; and lo, I am with you always, even to the end of the age." Matthew 28:20 (NASB)

[15] "If you love Me, you will keep My commandments." John 14:15 (NASB)

[10] "If you keep My commandments, you will abide in My love; just as I have kept My Father's commandments, and abide in His love." John 15:10 (NASB)

[48] "He who rejects Me, and does not receive My sayings, has one who judges him; the word I spoke is what will judge him at the last day." John 12:48 (NASB)

[23] Jesus answered and said to him, "If anyone loves Me, he will keep My word; and My Father will love him, and We will come to him, and make Our abode with him. [24] He who does not love Me does not keep My words; and the word which you hear is not Mine, but the Father's who sent Me." John 14:23-24 (NASB)

The terms of the covenant include not only obedience to Christ words, but also obedience to the words of His apostles:

[20] "Remember the word that I said to you, "A slave is not

greater than his master." If they persecuted Me, they will also persecute you; if they kept My word, they will keep yours also." John 15:20 (NASB)

[13] "But when He, the Spirit of truth, comes, He will guide you into all the truth; for He will not speak on His own initiative, but whatever He hears, He will speak; and He will disclose to you what is to come. [14] He will glorify Me; for He will take of Mine, and shall disclose it to you. [15] All things that the Father has are Mine; therefore I said that He takes of Mine, and will disclose it to you." John 16:13-15 (NASB)

[37] If anyone thinks he is a prophet or spiritual, let him recognize that the things which I write to you are the Lord's commandment. [38] But if anyone does not recognize this, he is not recognized. 1 Corinthians 14:37-38 (NASB)

[13] For this reason we also constantly thank God that when you received the word of God which you heard from us, you accepted it not as the word of men, but for what it really is, the word of God, which also performs its work in you who believe. 1 Thessalonians 2:13 (NASB)

[14] Therefore, beloved, since you look for these things, be diligent to be found by Him in peace, spotless and blameless, [15] and regard the patience of our Lord as salvation; just as also our beloved brother Paul, according to the wisdom given him, wrote to you, [16] as also in all his letters, speaking in them of these things, in which are some things hard to understand, which the untaught and unstable distort, as they do also the rest of the Scriptures, to their own destruction. 2 Peter 3:14-16 (NASB)

5. Blessings and Curses—The basic idea here is heaven or hell. The primary blessings are forgiveness of sins, salvation and eternal life by the grace of God through faith in the crucified and resurrected Christ (Ephesians 2:8-10). Christ calls people "blessed"

in the following passages: Matthew 5:3-11; 11:6; 13:16; 16:17; 24:46; Luke 6:20-22; 7:23; 10:23; 11:28; 12:37-38, 43; 14:14; John 13:17; 20:29. Paul calls people "blessed" in Romans 4:8 and 14:22. James calls people "blessed" in James 1:25. Peter calls people "blessed" in 1 Peter 3:14 and 4:14. John records that the following people are "blessed:" Revelation 1:3; 14:13; 16:15; 19:9; 20:6; 22:7, 14.

However, there are lists of sins which, if we do not repent, cause us to NOT go to Heaven (as examples, Matthew 15:19; Galatians 5:19-21; Colossians 3:5-9; 1 Corinthians 6:9-10; 1 Timothy 1:8-10). In addition, there is severe condemnation for a Christian who falls away (for example, 2 Peter 2:21-22; Luke 12:47; Hebrews 6:4-6; 10:26-27; James 4:17). Jesus will curse the disobedient at the Judgment (Matthew 25:41-44), but we must not curse anyone (James 3:9-10).

6. Oath-Swearing Ceremony—In Christian baptism, we are joined with Christ in His death, burial and resurrection. We are joined with Him in His bloody sacrifice on the cross (Romans 6:3-5). We identify with the life, the body and the blood of Christ in His one-time sacrifice for all people. Because of our critical union with Christ that occurs in baptism, we are also agreeing that such severe sufferings as our Savior endured should be borne by us if we fall away from this New Covenant.
7. Covenant Renewal—In Christianity, the Lord's Supper is the covenant renewal ceremony. The unleavened bread represents the body of Christ (Luke 22:19). The cup is the "blood of the covenant" (Matthew 26:28), and represents "the new covenant in my blood" (Luke 22:20; 1 Corinthians 11:25). We are to partake "in remembrance" of Christ (1 Corinthians 11:25).

Restorations of God's Covenant with Jesus Christ

In the previous chapters we explored the multiple restorations of covenants God made in the Old Testament. These restorations involved the Covenants with Adam, Noah, Abraham and Moses/Israel and David. As there is a vast wealth of biblical history spanning approximately 1.5 millennia from Abraham to Malachi, we were able to profit greatly and gain significant understanding of how God causes restoration of His Covenants.

This present chapter explores restorations of the New Covenant. However, the contents of the New Testament span only about 100 years. Therefore we do not have that vast wealth of biblical history following God's New Covenant with his Son Jesus Christ in the New Testament as we did with the Mosaic Covenant the Old Testament. Therefore, we will need to utilize both the New Testament as well as church history in order to see how God brings about restorations of the New Covenant.

The Apostles and New Testament Prophets as Restorers of the New Covenant

As Jesus was nearing His trial, death, burial, and resurrection in AD 30, He gave to His apostles specific and lengthy instructions and those are found in John chapters 13 through 17. Among those instructions Christ revealed that He would return to the Father, but would send the Holy Spirit to guide the apostles. The Holy Spirit would accomplish the following things in and through the apostles:

1. The Holy Spirit will teach the apostles all things (John 14:26),
2. Bring to the apostles' remembrance all that Christ said to them (John 14:26),
3. Bear witness about Christ (John 15:26),
4. Convict the world concerning sin, righteousness, and judgment (John 16:8),
5. Guide the apostles into all truth (John 16:13), and
6. Declare to the apostles the things that were to come (John 16:13).

Not only these, but Christ also confirmed the importance of the apostles' teachings in John 15:20 and 17:20. Since the apostles' teachings would be inspired by the Holy Spirit, their teachings would be as binding as Christ's own teachings, for, in fact, they were Christ's teachings (see also Galatians 4:14; 1 Thessalonians 2:13; 2 Peter 3:15-16; Matthew 10:20).

After Christ's resurrection from the dead, He was with the apostles for 40 days and taught them about the "kingdom of God" (Acts 1:1-3), which according to Matthew 16:18-19 included teaching about what Christ called "my church." Prior to his ascension to heaven, Christ charged the apostles with the great commission (Matthew 28:18-20; Mark 16:15-16; Luke 24:47). However, the continuing work and revelation of Christ through the Holy Spirit continued under the administration of the apostles in the first century. This is clear in Acts 1:1-3 where Luke records that the gospel he had written was only the beginning of what Jesus "began to do and teach." Obviously, Christ continued to "do and to teach" even after His ascension through the Holy Spirit to His apostles. Thus, the apostles became not only those who taught the divine revelation of Christ in the New Covenant, but also those who fully communicated "all truth" in the New Covenant by their constant teaching, preaching, and writing. By this same apostolic ministry the New Covenant was continually and fully restored during their lives.

After Peter preached the first Gospel sermon (Acts 2:1-41), the people responded and what Jesus called "my church" was founded with about 3000 members. Beginning in AD 30, this continuing great commission was to be accomplished through a preaching ministry that first started in Jerusalem, then spread to Judea and Samaria, and then to the ends of the earth (Acts 1:8). This spreading of the Gospel was highly successful, and churches were successfully planted by the apostles and others throughout the known world.

Unfortunately, during the first 30-40 years after Christ gave the great commission, multiple problems arose in many churches. Examples of these included Jewish and pagan oppositions as follows:

1. Jewish opposition and persecution (Acts chapters 4:1 to 9:12; chapter 16; chapters 21 to 26; also see 13:50; 14:2, 5, 19; 17:5-9, 13; 18:12-17)
2. Judaizing teachers within the church (for example, Acts 15; Galatians; Romans; Hebrews)
3. Roman political opposition and persecution (for example, Acts chapters 24 through 28; see also Acts 14:5; 16:37)

4. Pagan religious opposition (Acts 13:8-11; 16:37; 17:32; 19:23-34)

In fact, opposition and persecution by Jewish, Roman, and pagan interests would continue in a fierce manner for a much longer period of time. Even after the destruction of Jerusalem in AD 70, the Jews joined the pagan Romans in their persecution of Christians [for example, see The Martyrdom of Polycarp, written in about AD 156, which you can read online (Kirby, 2001-2011)]. Intermittent and at times severe Roman persecution of Christians continued until the Roman Emperor Constantine in AD 313 declared tolerance for all religions in the Edict of Milan.

Therefore, in the midst of this persecution, the New Testament documents were written to continue the apostles' witness to all peoples. Now concerning when the New Testament was written, F. F. Bruce offers the following dates for these writings:

1. Matthew was written shortly after AD 70
2. Mark was written in about AD 64
3. Luke was written before AD 70
4. John was written approximately AD 90-100

   Bruce remarks that many would have been alive who could have remembered the events that were presented in the Gospels. More to the point, there is no evidence in the first century literature that the Jews could objectively refute anything that Jesus said, any miracle that Jesus performed, or Jesus' resurrection from the dead.

5. Acts was written in about AD 62
6. The Thirteen Pauline epistles:
   a. Galatians was written about AD 48
   b. 1 & 2 Thessalonians was written about AD 50
   c. 1 & 2 Corinthians was written about AD 54-56
   d. Romans was written about AD 57
   e. Philippians, Colossians, Philemon, & Ephesians were written about AD 60
   f. Pastoral Epistles were written about AD 63-65

Regarding an overview and documentation for the remainder, Bruce says the following:

> The New Testament was complete, or substantially complete, by AD 100, the majority of the writings being in existence 20 to 40 years before this. (Bruce, 1943, 1946, 1950, 1960, 1981, pp. 6-8)

Therefore, the New Covenant was preached from AD 30 onward. The written documents collectively known as the New Testament were published about one generation afterwards, and that entire process continually restored the New Covenant in the first century AD.

What follows in the next chapters is a review of the New Testament for the purpose of rediscovering the New Covenant that we might restore it in our own day. There are synopses and reflections on Gospels, Acts and the Pauline Epistles. The purpose is to look at the big picture of these books. Many Christians have little actual knowledge of what the New Testament says. Rather, they have been exposed to relatively few verses, but have never read the New Testament so that it can speak its own message to them. My hope is that these synopses will encourage the reader to read again, or read for the first time the New Testament, which is the New Covenant. Then it is my hope and prayer that the reader may the restore the teachings of the New Covenant to his/her own life, and also to the church.

Study Questions

1. Was the New Covenant prophesied by the Old Testament prophets?
2. Explain how Christ Himself is the New Covenant (Isaiah 42:6-7; 49:8).
3. Must we have a trusting faith in God and obey His commandments in the New Covenant?
4. Is it true that there are blessings (heaven) and curses (hell) in the New Covenant that apply to all people?
5. Explain what happens when we are baptized, how this is equivalent to an oath-swearing ceremony, and what penalties await us if we break covenant with God.
6. How is the New Covenant renewed or restored in the weekly partaking of the Lord's Supper? How does this relate to Christ Himself being the New Covenant? What is implied in the case of a Christian who purposefully avoids the weekly Lord's Supper?
7. By what date were all the New Testament documents written?
8. Do all the New Testament books serve the function of continually restoring the New Covenant?
9. Did the apostles speak and write the words of God or the words of men? Must we obey Christ? Must we obey the apostles? Defend your answers with Scriptures.

Chapter 7

The New Covenant—The Gospels

The Gospels as the Cornerstone of Restored Faith

Matthew and John were apostles and so their Gospels are apostolic. Luke was clearly inspired in his writing of Luke and Acts, and because of his loyal and constant association with the apostle Paul, Luke was undoubtedly influenced by what Paul called "my gospel" (for example, see "new covenant" in Luke 22:20 and 1 Corinthians 11:25; for "my gospel," see Romans 2:16; 16:25; 2 Timothy 2:8). Origen (AD 185-254), the successor of Clement at the Catechetical School of Alexandria, also commented on Luke, calling it the third Gospel which was commended by Paul (Pamphilus, 1997, p. 6:25.6). Mark was also inspired in his writing of the Gospel of Mark. Mark was very close to Peter, and Peter called Mark his son (1 Peter 5:13). Irenaeus (died AD 202) also commented on the relationships of the apostles to both Mark and Luke in the following manner:

> The opinion of the apostles, therefore, and of those (Mark's and Luke's) who learned from their words, concerning God, has been made manifest. (Irenaeus, 1997)

Clement of Alexandria (c AD 150-215) gives the following information on Mark:

> Mark, the follower of Peter, while Peter publicly preached the Gospel at Rome before some of Caesar's equites, and adduced many testimonies to Christ, in order that thereby they might be able to commit to memory what was spoken, of what was spoken by Peter wrote entirely what is called the Gospel according to Mark. (Clemens, 1997)

Therefore, the Gospels are the apostolic witnesses to the life of Christ. Within these we find an extraordinary amount of evidence regarding Christ. The primary purpose of the Gospels is to serve as a legal defense for Christ. Yes, there are other very important mandates for us, such as obeying all that He commanded (Matthew 28:20), and living according to His example as much as a human being possibly can. The Sermon on the Mount (Matthew 5 to 7) is an excellent summary of Christ's teachings and these must be studied by the Christian so the terms of the New Covenant are fully understood and obeyed. My review of the Sermon on the Mount and on Christ as our example have been previously published (Vadney, 2010).

The idea of the Gospels being a legal defense for Christ comes from Christ Himself in John 5:30-47. In this passage, Jesus outlines the witnesses who affirm He is the Christ, the Son of God.

Christ bears witness about Himself (John 5:30-31)

As examples, see John 8:13-14; 18:21, 37; Matthew 16:16-18, 27; 24:30-31; 26:63-64; 27:11; Mark 14:61; 15:2; 16:19; Luke 23:1-3. Jesus gave us much information about Himself in the Gospels. In Matthew 11:29-30, Jesus is gentle and lowly in heart. In Matthew 16:13-19, Jesus is the Christ, the Son of the Living God. In Matthew 16:28; 19:28-30; Jesus is the Son of Man (see Daniel 7:13-14). Jesus is the King (John 18:36-37). Jesus is the Son of God (Mark 14:61-62).

There are seven "I am" sayings of Jesus in the Gospel of John that helps us understand who He is and what He does for us. These are as follows:

1. I am the bread of life (John 6:35, 48).
2. I am the light of the world (John 8:12; 9:5).
3. Before Abraham was, I am (John 8:58).
4. I am the good shepherd (John 10:11).
5. I am the resurrection and the life (John 11:25).
6. I am the way, the truth, and the life (John 14:6).
7. I am the true vine (John 15:1).

John the Baptist bears witness about Christ (John 5:32-35)

John the Baptist testifies that Jesus is the Lamb of God and the Son of God (John 1:29-34).

Christ's miracles testify that He is the Son of God (John 5:36)

The apostle John organized his Gospel differently than the synoptic Gospels (Matthew, Mark, and Luke). He displayed the following "signs" of Christ:

1. Jesus changes the water to wine (John 2:1-11).
2. Jesus heals the nobleman's son (John 4:46-54).
3. Jesus heals the impotent man, who had been an invalid for 38 years (John 5:1-9).
4. Jesus feeds 5000 men (John 6:1-14).
5. Jesus walks on water (John 6:16-21).
6. Jesus, on the Sabbath, heals a man born blind (John 9:1-12).
7. Jesus raises Lazarus from the dead (John 11:1-46).

The miracles of Jesus found in Matthew, Mark and Luke and Acts are very numerous. There were miracles before the conception of Jesus, miracles during His gestation, miracles during His infancy, countless miracles during His ministry, miracles while He was on the cross, and the foremost miracles were shown in His resurrection and His miraculous ascension. The following list is an attempt to catalogue these events so that the reader may be able to see the vast scope of the miraculous phenomena associated with the Jesus Christ, the Son of the Living God.

1. Promise of John the Baptist's birth—his parents were very old and thus conception, successful pregnancy and safe delivery were "impossible" (Luke 1:5-25)
2. Miraculous conception of Jesus (Matthew 1:18-25)
3. Announcement to Mary regarding having a son though she was a virgin (Luke 1:26-38)
4. Visit of the Magi—God must have told them (Matthew 2:1-12)
5. Mary's visit to Elizabeth—Elizabeth knows already of Mary's miraculous conception (Luke 1:39-56)
6. Birth of John the Baptist—his father finally spoke and he prophesied (Luke 1:57-80)
7. Birth of Jesus—announced by angels unto shepherds (Luke 2:1-20)
8. Circumcision of Jesus and Presentation—Simeon already knew Jesus was the Christ (Luke 2:21-40)
9. Flight into Egypt and return (Matthew 2:13-23)
10. Jesus at 12 years old—He already knows the identity of His Father (Luke 2:41-52)
11. Baptism of Jesus—The Holy Spirit descends on Jesus and the Father says "This is my beloved Son" (Matthew 3:13-17; Mark 1:9-11; Luke 3:21-22)
12. Rejection at Nazareth—Jesus healed some sick people; the people of Nazareth intended to kill Him but he passed through their midst (Matthew 13:53-58; Mark 6:1-6)
13. Jesus in the Synagogue at Capernaum—Jesus healed a man with an unclean spirit (demon), and He commanded unclean spirits and they obeyed Him (Mark 1:21-28; Luke 4:31-37)
14. Healing of Peter's mother-in-law (Matthew 8:14-15; Mark 1:29-31; Luke 4:38-39)
15. The sick healed at evening—included casting out demons and healing those with various diseases (Matthew 8:16-17; Mark 1:32-34; Luke 4:40-41)

16. Preaching journey in Galilee—healed every disease and infirmity, cast out demons, and cured various diseases including epileptics and paralytics (Matthew 4:23-25; Mark 1:39)
17. Miraculous catch of fish (Luke 5:1-11)
18. Healing of a leper (Matthew 8:1-4; Mark 1:40-44; Luke 5:12-16)
19. Healing of the Centurion's servant—Jesus does so by distance, never seeing the servant (Matthew 8:5-13; Luke 7:1-10)
20. Calming the storm (Matthew 8:23-27; Mark 4:38-41; Luke 8:22-25)
21. Healing the two Gadarene Demoniacs (Matthew 8:28-34; Mark 5:1-20; Luke 8:26-39)
22. Healing the paralytic—"your sins are forgiven" (Matthew 9:1-8; Mark 2:1-12; Luke 5:17-26)
23. Resurrection of Jairus' daughter (Matthew 9:18, 19, 23-26; Mark 5:21-24, 35-43; Luke 8:41-42, 49-56)
24. Healing of a woman with a chronic discharge of blood (Matthew 9:20-22; Mark 5: 25-34; Luke 8:43-48)
25. Two blind men healed (Matthew 9:27-31)
26. Healing of a mute demoniac (Matthew 9:32-34)
27. Limited Commission of the 12—Jesus gave the 12 apostles authority to heal the sick, raise the dead, cleanse the lepers, and cast out demons; they were successful in doing so (Matthew 10:5-32; Luke 9:1-6)
28. Jesus sends out the 72—Jesus commanded the 72 to heal the sick and to cast out demons (Luke 10:1-20)
29. Future persecutions of the 12—Jesus promised the "Spirit of your Father speaking through you" (Matthew 10:16-23; Mark 13:11; Luke 21:15)
30. Jesus performed multiple miracles for John the Baptist's disciples—the blind received sight, lame walked, lepers cleansed, deaf heard, dead are raised up, poor had good news preached to them (Matthew 11:2-6; Luke 7:18-23)
31. Healing of the man with the withered hand—question of healing on the Sabbath (Matthew 12:9-14; Mark 3:1-6; Luke 6:6-11)
32. Jesus healed multitudes (Matthew 12:15; Mark 3:7-12; Luke 6:17-19)
33. Resurrection of the widow's son at Nain (Luke 7:11-17)

34. Healing the blind and dumb demoniac (Matthew 12:22-24; Luke 11:14-16)
35. Feeding of the 5,000 (Matthew 14:13-21; Mark 6:30-44; Luke 9:10-17)
36. Walking on the water (Matthew 14:22-33; Mark 6:45-52)
37. Healings at Gennesaret (Matthew 14:34-36; Mark 6:53-56)
38. Healing of the Syrophoenician woman's daughter—cast out a demon from a distance (Matthew 15:21-28; Mark 7:24-30)
39. Healing of many who were lame, blind, mute, etc. (Matthew 15:29-31)
40. Healing of a deaf man who had an impediment of speech (Mark 8:31-37)
41. Feeding the 4,000 (Matthew 15:32-39; Mark 8:1-10)
42. Healing of the blind man of Bethsaida (Mark 8:22-26)
43. The Transfiguration of Christ (Matthew 17:1-8; Mark 9:2-8; Luke 9:28-36)
44. Jesus healed an epileptic boy (Matthew 17:14-21; Mark 9:14-29; Luke 9:37-43)
45. The fish with the Temple tax payment (Matthew 17:24-27)
46. The strange exorcist not associated with the 12 apostles—God must have given him his power (Mark 9:38-41; Luke 9:49-50)
47. Healing of the woman with a disabling spirit—on the Sabbath (Luke 13:10-17)
48. Healing of a man with dropsy—on the Sabbath (Luke 14:1-6)
49. Healings of the 10 lepers (Luke 17:11-19)
50. Healing of blind Bartimaeus and another blind man (Matthew 20:29-34; Mark 10:46-52; Luke 18:35-43)
51. Healings of the blind and lame in the Temple (Matthew 21:14)
52. Cursing of the fig tree (Matthew 21:18-22; Mark 11:12-14; 20-25)
53. Prophecies fulfilled about Jesus even while He was on the cross (see prophecies)
54. Resurrections of many saints occurred when Jesus died on the cross (Matthew 27:52-53)
55. Resurrection and appearances of Jesus Christ:
    a. Guards (Matthew 28:1-4)
    b. Mary Magdalene (Mark 16:9)

c. Disciples on the road to Emmaus (Luke 24:13-35)
d. Disciples in Jerusalem (Luke 24:36-39)
e. Ascension (Luke 24:50-53; Acts 1:6-11)

Thus, there are more than 50 incidences describing the various mighty works and wonders that Jesus did or that were associated with Him. All these evidences demonstrate that He is the Christ, the Son of the Living God.

The apostle John makes it clear that Jesus did far more miracles than what has been recorded:

> [30] Therefore many other signs Jesus also performed in the presence of the disciples, which are not written in this book; [31] but these have been written so that you may believe that Jesus is the Christ, the Son of God; and that believing you may have life in His name. John 20:30-31 (NASB)

> [25] And there are also many other things which Jesus did, which if they were written in detail, I suppose that even the world itself would not contain the books that would be written. John 21:25 (NASB)

The Father bears witness about Christ (John 5:37-38)

The Father testifies that Jesus is His Son at Christ's baptism (Matthew 3:13-17) and at Christ's transfiguration (Matthew 17:1-7; Mark 9:2-7; Luke 9:28-36).

The Scriptures bear witness about Christ (John 5:39)

Liberal theology scholars, unbelieving Jews, people of Islam and atheists forcefully deny that any prophecy of the Old Testament refers to Jesus. Nevertheless, Luke writes this concerning what Jesus said about Himself: "And beginning with Moses and all the Prophets, he interpreted to them in all the Scriptures the things concerning himself." (Luke 24:27 ESV). Luke also quotes Jesus directly when he said, "…

everything written about me in the Law of Moses and the Prophets and the Psalms must be fulfilled." (Luke 24:44 ESV). Therefore, we must choose between those who deny the teachings of Christ versus those who affirm His teachings on this subject. I choose the teachings of my Lord and Savior, Jesus Christ, the Son of the Living God.

Now it is important for us to understand that the Old Testament prophets did not fully understand all that God commanded them to proclaim to the people. The prophets were God's mouthpiece, and they were faithful in proclaiming everything, even those things that they didn't fully understand. For example, consider Daniel's visions, and how he repeatedly asked the angels to explain the prophecies to him (Daniel 7:16, 19; 8:15-16, 27; 9:22; 12:8). Even after these explanations, Daniel didn't always understand the visions or the interpretations of those visions.

Peter's insight into the minds of the prophets is helpful:

> [10] As to this salvation, the prophets who prophesied of the grace that would come to you made careful searches and inquiries, [11] seeking to know what person or time the Spirit of Christ within them was indicating as He predicted the sufferings of Christ and the glories to follow. [12] It was revealed to them that they were not serving themselves, but you, in these things which now have been announced to you through those who preached the gospel to you by the Holy Spirit sent from heaven—things into which angels long to look. 1 Peter 1:10-12 (NASB)

Therefore, we must rely heavily on the understanding of Christ and His apostles regarding these Old Testament prophecies about Christ. Jesus promised that the Holy Spirit would guide his apostles into all truth (John 16:13). In addition, Jesus clearly explained to His apostles how the "Law of Moses and the Prophets and the Psalms" (Luke 24:44-47) all spoke of Him.

The following table presents the references to prophecies regarding Christ as found in the Gospels and Acts. Although there are hundreds more in the Old Testament, these are clearly referenced in the Gospels and Acts, so that is why I have included them in this table:

Events	*OT Prophecy*	*NT Fulfillment*
Virgin Birth	Isa 7:14	Matt 1:18-23
Called out of Egypt	Hosea 11:1	Matt 2:14-15
Born in Bethlehem	Micah 5:2	Matt 2:3-6
Slaughter of infants	Jer 31:15	Matt 2:17-18
Called a Nazarene, a term of scorn (see also the note at the end of the table)	Isa 11:1 (Hebrew); John 1:45-46; Isa 53:3; Ps 22:6	Matt 2:23
John the Baptist would prepare the way	Isa 40:3-5	Matt 3:3
He would fulfill all righteousness	Isa 9:7; 11:4-5; 16:5; 32:1, 15-17	Matt 3:15
He would live in Capernaum	Isa 9:1-2	Matt 4:14-16
He would cast out demons and heal	Isa 53:4	Matt 8:16-17
His quiet and gentle nature	Isa 42:1-3	Matt 12:15-17
People would not understand or believe him	Isa 6:9-10; 53:1	Matt 13:10-15; John 12:37-40
He would preach using parables	Ps 78:2	Matt 13:34-35
His vicarious death to be fulfilled	Isa 53:5-10	Matt 26:54, 56
His betrayal price; potter's field	Jer 18:1-6; 19:1-14; Zech 11:13	Matt 27:3-7
His message & healings predicted	Isa 61:1-2	Luke 4:16-21
Destruction of Jerusalem predicted	Daniel 9:26-27	Luke 21:20-24
Thought to be a transgressor	Isa 53:12	Luke 22:36-38
He would be exalted to the right hand of God	Ps 110:1	Luke 20:41-44

Events	***OT Prophecy***	***NT fulfillment***
Isaiah saw Him and prophesied His glory	Isa 6:1-10; 53:1	John 12:38-41
A close disciple would betray Him	Ps 41:9	John 13:18; 17:12
They would hate/reject Christ despite evidence	Ps 35:19; 69:4	John 15:23-25
They would divide and cast lots for his clothing	Ps 22:18	John 19:23-24
He would thirst & be given sour wine to drink	Ps 69:21	John 19:28
While on the cross, they would not break his legs but would pierce him	Ex 12:46; Num 9:12; Ps 34:20; Zech 12:10	John 19:31-37
He would be called the Son of God	Ps 2:7	Acts 13:33
He would be permanently raised from the dead	Is 53:12; Ps 16:10	Acts 13:34-35
Jesus is the Prophet whom Moses prophesied would come; we must obey Him	Deut 18:15, 18, 19	Acts 3:22

("Nazareth" is derived from the Hebrew *ne ser*, which is translated "branch" in Isaiah 11:1. (Dosker, Nazarene, 1939, 1956))

Liberal theological scholars say these prophecies cited in the Gospels and Acts cannot refer to Christ because the context in each case indicates it must refer to someone at the time the Old Testament book was written. Clearly this may be the case, i.e., that some of these prophecies do refer to a fulfillment at the time it was written. However, since Christ and the apostles say that these Scriptures speak of fulfillment in Jesus, then they are fulfilled in Jesus. In some instances we may need to view these prophecies of Christ as a "double fulfillment," or a "fuller sense fulfillment" or even a "type fulfillment" (Hosea 11:1). The point is the gospel writers were not telling us lies, but were saying on the authority of

Christ's revelation to them (Luke 24:25-27, 44-47) that these prophecies were fulfilled in Christ.

I have shown only 27 prophecies. However, Richard Rogers said that there were over 1500 Old Testament prophecies about Christ (Rogers, 2002, p. 1). Ted Stewart documents 95 Old Testament prophecies that fulfill 80 different aspects of Christ's life, including his nature, birth, youth, forerunner, roles, life, ministry, rejection, death, resurrection, and ascension (Stewart, 2001, p. 191). Unfortunately, many in the Western world now deny these, for there is a veil over their hearts just as there was a veil over the hearts of the unbelieving Jews in the first century (2 Corinthians 3:12-18).

I invite you to think like Christ and His apostles about these Old Testament prophecies about our Lord and Savior. Realize that it was the Spirit of Christ who was in those Old Testament prophets, and they knew that Christ would suffer and then be glorified (1 Peter 1:10-12). But the picture was not perfectly clear until Christ came. Open your minds and your hearts and remove the veil. See the Old Testament explode with testimony about Christ, just as the apostles did. Learn like the apostles from Jesus, that the Psalms, Prophets, and the Law of Moses all bear witness to Christ. Rejoice as you realize that it is Christ who is the golden thread that holds all of God's revelation in the Bible together.

Moses bears witness about Christ (John 5:45-47)

Although this witness is a subset of those Old Testament Prophecies about Christ as mentioned above, Christ separates Moses' prophecy as a special interest, saying, "he wrote of me" (John 5:46). This is because Moses was so special to the Jews, and a reference from what Moses said could not be easily dismissed. Jesus clearly was referring to Numbers 21:9 (see John 3:14-15) and Deuteronomy 18:15-19 (see Luke 24:27; Acts 3:22; 7:37). However, there were prophecies about Jesus in Genesis too. Consider the following passages: Genesis 3:15; 12:3; 26:4; 28:12 (John 1:51); Genesis 49:10. Genesis was attributed to Moses also, so these would be additional prophecies from Moses about Christ. There are also "types" that are fulfilled in Christ from Moses such as the bronze serpent (Numbers 21:9; John 3:14).

REFLECTIONS

We should understand that the Gospels are the apostolic witnesses concerning Christ. We should consider the evidence that Christ has outlined for us and study it well because it is wonderful and it builds faith. Don't let any liberal theologian or any other adversary to the biblical record ruin your faith with their attacks on this evidence. In fact, since this evidence is true, it will build faith if you study it well and become convinced regarding this evidence.

The Gospels are the apostolic witnesses concerning the life of Christ. Each time these Gospels are read there is generated either belief or unbelief. If ours is a response of belief and obedience to Christ, then we become part of God's on-going restoration of the New Covenant, and we are then Christians according to God's order rather than to man's order. It is implausible to think one can be called a Christian and not believe in these fundamental facts that the Gospels present, including the six lines of evidence that Christ Himself set firmly before us as fact.

Study Questions

1. Explain why all the Gospels, i.e., Matthew, Mark, Luke, and John, are considered apostolic witnesses to the life of Christ.
2. Explain how the Gospels are a legal defense for Jesus as being the Christ, the Son of God.
3. Who or what are the six witnesses Christ calls for His defense?
4. What are the famous seven "I am" statements by Christ regarding Himself, and what do these teach us about Him?
5. What does John the Baptist say about Christ?
6. Many miracles of Christ are found in the gospels. Are these all of the miracles Christ performed, or are there more?
7. At what two events did the Father give His witness about Christ?
8. Did Jesus say that many Old Testament prophecies speak of Him?
9. The last witness Jesus calls is Moses. Did Moses prophesy about Christ?

Chapter 8

New Covenant—Acts

Acts as a Restoration Pattern for Conversion

Acts is the Christian's early church history book. It describes the start and the spread of Christianity from Jerusalem, Judea, Samaria, and to the ends of the earth (Acts 1:8). The overall pattern is that wherever the Gospel was preached, the church was established in that location.

There are multiple examples of conversions detailed in Acts. Therefore, by reading Acts, a person can see for himself/herself how one becomes a Christian under the oversight of the apostles. First, let us consider the commands of Christ our Lord regarding this issue, then consider the faithful implementation of Christ's commands by the apostles.

After Christ was raised from the dead, an event attested to by not only the apostles, but by over 500 people to whom He revealed Himself (1 Corinthians 15:5-8), He charged His apostles with the great commission:

> [18] And Jesus came up and spoke to them, saying, "All authority has been given to Me in heaven and on earth. [19] Go therefore and make disciples of all the nations, baptizing them in the name of the Father and the Son and the Holy Spirit, [20] teaching them to

observe all that I commanded you; and lo, I am with you always, even to the end of the age." Matthew 28:18-20 (NASB) (Spoken in Galilee on a mountain by Jesus to the apostles)

[15] And He said to them, "Go into all the world and preach the gospel to all creation. [16] He who has believed and has been baptized shall be saved; but he who has disbelieved shall be condemned." Mark 16:15-16 (NASB) (Spoken near Jerusalem by Jesus to the apostles.)

[44] Now He said to them, "These are My words which I spoke to you while I was still with you, that all things which are written about Me in the Law of Moses and the Prophets and the Psalms must be fulfilled." [45] Then He opened their minds to understand the Scriptures, [46] and He said to them, "Thus it is written, that the Christ would suffer and rise again from the dead the third day, [47] and that repentance for forgiveness of sins would be proclaimed in His name to all the nations, beginning from Jerusalem. [48] You are witnesses of these things. [49] And behold, I am sending forth the promise of My Father upon you; but you are to stay in the city until you are clothed with power from on high." Luke 24:44-49 (NASB) (Spoken near Jerusalem by Jesus to the apostles.)

[19] So when it was evening on that day, the first day of the week, and when the doors were shut where the disciples were, for fear of the Jews, Jesus came and stood in their midst and said to them, "Peace be with you." [20] And when He had said this, He showed them both His hands and His side. The disciples then rejoiced when they saw the Lord. [21] So Jesus said to them again, "Peace be with you; as the Father has sent Me, I also send you." [22] And when He had said this, He breathed on them and said to them, "Receive the Holy Spirit. [23] If you forgive the sins of any, their sins have been forgiven them; if you retain the sins of any, they have been retained." John 20:19-23 (NASB) (Spoken in or near Jerusalem by Jesus to the apostles.)

Christ's command as found in Matthew is prefaced by His solemn statement that "All authority has been given to Me in heaven and on earth." Some say that Christ never said anything like this before and doubt that He could or would make such a claim. However, Christ did say such things before (Matthew 11:27; John 3:35; 13:3; 17:2), and such was also prophesied about Him (Daniel 7:13-14). His statements in Galilee stressed the making and teaching of disciples of all nations. The apostles were also commanded to baptize these disciples. Thus, Jesus commanded an informed faith and baptism for one to become a Christian.

Christ's commands as found in Mark 16:16 are challenged by many because it is part of a controversial ending of Mark which is not found in the oldest of documents. I will not present any apology regarding this passage at this time. However, it is clear that the demands of Christ concerning making Christians in this disputed passage are not different than what is found in Matthew. Like Matthew, faith and baptism are commanded here in Mark. Mark is more explicit in that if these are not done, one will be condemned. However, not following the explicit commands of God has always been viewed as a great sin in both the Old and New Testaments. Can we really expect to be saved if we do not obey Christ's commands? The Western peoples live in a dream world where their god is never condemning and always loving, and their god will save everyone regardless of whether they are Christians or not, and their god would never send anyone, including Satan, into everlasting punishment. They say that all religions pray to the same god. But this is neither the God nor the faith of the New Testament. Such idolatry is no different in kind to the idolatry of the Orient, India or Africa. We must believe what Christ commanded the apostles to preach, and we must obey Christ's commands given through His faithful apostles.

> [6] Jesus said to him, "I am the way, and the truth, and the life; no one comes to the Father but through Me." John 14:6 (NASB)

> [44] And Jesus cried out and said, "He who believes in Me, does not believe in Me but in Him who sent Me. [45] He who sees Me sees the One who sent Me. [46] I have come as Light into the world, so that everyone who believes in Me will not remain in darkness. [47] If anyone hears My sayings and does not keep them, I do not judge him; for I did not come to judge the world, but to save the world.

> [48] He who rejects Me and does not receive My sayings, has one who judges him; the word I spoke is what will judge him at the last day. [49] For I did not speak on My own initiative, but the Father Himself who sent Me has given Me a commandment as to what to say and what to speak. [50] I know that His commandment is eternal life; therefore the things I speak, I speak just as the Father has told Me." John 12:44-50 (NASB)

Christ's command as found in Luke stresses teaching the death and resurrection of Christ. Clearly this is the major part of the informed faith God wants of anyone who desires to become a Christian. Also Luke stresses the "repentance for the forgiveness of sins." Without repentance, that is, a radical change in behavior that abandons all sin, it is impossible to become a Christian in the sight of God.

John stresses Christ sending the apostles in the same manner that God sent Christ. Not only this, but John also stresses the authority Christ gave the apostles, even to the point of forgiving or not forgiving sins. Jesus had previously cursed the fruitless fig tree (Matthew 21:18-19; Mark 11:12-14) as an object lesson to the apostles and to us as well. It was His only miracle with a negative connotation. The message is that we must be fruitful and ready to meet our Savior when He comes, even if we consider the time of His coming "unseasonable" or "inconvenient," or we too will be cursed. In like manner the apostle Peter met the crafty, cunning, deceptive, misleading, and dishonest Ananias and Sapphira with a lethal message (Acts 5:1-11). In like manner also, the power-hungry, envious, and covetous Simon the Magician of Samaria approached Peter wanting to buy the ability to pass the Holy Spirit to others by the laying on of his hands, just as he had seen the apostles Peter and John do (Acts 8:14-24). Peter rebuked him also with the most severe of terms. These three, Ananias, Sapphira, and Simon the Magician were all Christians. Yet, they still had to respect and obey the apostles. Therefore, we must stand in awe of the power that Christ gave the apostles. It was power not only to build up, but even to destroy, just as Christ had destroyed the fig tree because it had no fruit.

Therefore, we see clearly that Jesus commanded faith, repentance, and baptism for one to become a Christian. He also gave the apostles substantial authority in delivering this message. Now let us turn our attention to Acts to see how the faithful apostles delivered those commands to the people. The following is a table of the notable conversions in Acts and what those individuals did to become Christians. Some of these elements are implied from the context, but most are explicit from the text. Top Code: Bel= believe, Rep=repent, Con=Confess, Bap= Baptism; code for data: C=context, √=present

People	***Scripture***	***Bel***	***Rep***	***Con***	***Bap***
Jews in Jerusalem	Acts 2:38-41	C	√		√
Jews in Jerusalem	Acts 4:4	√			
Samaritans	Acts 8:12-13	√			√
Ethiopian Eunuch	Acts 8:30-39	C			√
Saul (Paul)	Acts 9:1-18; 22:6-16; 26:12-18	C	C	C	√
In Jopa	Acts 9:42	√			
Cornelius	Acts 10:1-48	C		C	√
In Antioch	Acts 11:19-26	√	C		C
Proconsul in Paphos	Acts 13:6-12	√			
In Antioch of Pisidia	Acts 13:48	√			
Iconium	Acts 14:1-6	√			
Lystra	Acts 14:19-22	√			
Gentiles	Acts 15:19	C	C		
Lydia	Acts 16:11-15	√			√
Philippian Jailer	Acts 16:25-34	√	C		√
Berea	Acts 17:12	√			
Athens	Acts 17:16-34	√			
Corinth	Acts 18:8	√			√
Ephesus	Acts 19:1-6	C			√
Jews in Jerusalem	Acts 21:20	√			

People	***Scripture***	***Bel***	***Rep***	***Con***	***Bap***
Gentiles, abroad in the empire	Acts 21:25	√			
Christians	Acts 22:19	√			
All People	Acts 26:20	C	√		

This table shows 23 instances of conversion or historical statements made about conversion. Faith is always present, either in the context or explicitly within the text. Faith is central to conversion. Without faith we cannot please God (Hebrews 11:6). Baptism is mentioned in 9 of these references. Repentance is mentioned or implied in the context in 6 instances. Confession of faith in Jesus is implied in two.

Many of the instances where baptism is not mentioned are very brief conversion accounts. It appears that "faith" in these situations is a summary description of people becoming Christians. This is explicitly so in the last three scriptures listed. These three are all recalling past events. Historically, "belief" encapsulates both repentance and baptism. Repentance, or turning to God and away from sin, was preached by Peter in Acts 2:38. It was also Paul's description of what he had been preaching throughout his ministry.

In Acts, the confession of faith in Christ is implied rather than stated in only two cases. Otherwise, the confession of the Ethiopian Eunuch in Acts 8:37 is problematic. The majority of modern English translations either put this verse in brackets, in italics, or in a footnote. This is to indicate that Acts 8:37 is not found in the oldest and most reliable Greek manuscripts. Textual scholars agree that Acts 8:37 was a very early interpolation, that is, it was added to the Greek text at an early time. Acts 8:37 was first referenced by Irenaeus (AD 170-210) and also by Cyprian (AD 200-258). Erasmus (AD 1446-1536) included it in his Greek text, and because of this it was included in the KJV (Reese, 1976, 2002, pp. 340-341).

However, even if Acts 8:37 is an interpolation, we should not think that confession of our faith in Christ is not part of our conversion. When Jesus asked His apostles who they thought He was, Peter answered with the great confession, "You are the Christ, the Son of the Living God"

(Matthew 16:16). In Matthew 16:18, Jesus says of Peter's confession, "...upon on this rock I will build my church...." Therefore, our confession that "Jesus is the Christ, the Son of God" is very pleasing to God. If we are not willing to acknowledge/confess Christ before men, Christ will deny us before His Father in heaven (Matthew 10:32-33). Belief in Christ and confession with our mouth that Jesus is Lord is essential for our salvation (Romans 10:9-10). Just as Jesus made that good confession regarding who He was before Jewish leaders (Luke 22:70) and Pontius Pilate (Matthew 27:11; John 18:37), so also Timothy made that good confession of who Jesus was in the presence of many witnesses (1 Timothy 6:12-14). This confession is a confession of the gospel or good news concerning Christ (2 Corinthians 9:13; Hebrews 3:1; 4:14; 10:23).

From the practical side, when a person expresses a desire to be baptized, the one who baptizes this person would be negligent if he did not assure himself about the person's faith. There are people who want to be baptized to please a parent or a spouse, but not because they believe in Christ. They must be baptized for the right reason. They should not be baptized for the wrong reason. Lipscomb offers this sage advice:

> Every one who baptizes should demand the assurance of faith. The direct way to assure this is to confess faith in Christ. This, I take it, beyond doubt, was the custom in the early ages of the church, and the custom was probably the cause of the interpolation. (Lipscomb, 1896, pp. 94-95)

Acts as a Restoration Pattern for The Church

Therefore, we have seen in Acts how we must become Christians, and how faithful the apostles were to Christ's charge in this matter. In addition we gain substantial understanding about the Church in Acts, and I will attempt to summarize this now.

The Establishment and the Nature of the New Testament Church

First, we find that Christ's command regarding the establishment and the spread of the Gospel (Acts 1:8) was fulfilled in a most faithful manner by the apostles. In this passage, Christ promises that the apostles would "receive power when the Holy Spirit has come upon you." This occurred on the day of Pentecost in Acts 2:1-4, and the manifestation of the Holy Spirit was that the apostles spoke in tongues they had never learned (Acts 2:6, 11). These were not "unknown" tongues. Rather, these tongues were real languages spoken and clearly heard by real people. Peter then delivered his sermon and preached the Gospel of Christ. He did this by citing prophecies in Joel 2:28-32, Psalms 16:8-11, and Psalms 110:1. These were prophecies about the coming of the New Covenant and the coming of the Messiah which were fulfilled in Christ. Peter convicted the Jews, who were the very Jews who demanded that Pontius Pilate, the governor, crucify Jesus. They had killed the Christ, but God had raised Him up again. Peter's commands to "Repent and be baptized" were accepted and about 3,000 people were baptized and added that day. These people were added to Christ, were added to the apostles, and were added to the church.

This gathering of these Jewish Christians in Acts 2 was called the "church" in Acts 5:11. The word "church" is spoken three times in the Gospels by Christ (Matthew 16:18; 18:17 [x2]) and sixteen times in Acts (Acts 5:11; 8:1, 3; 9:31; 11:22, 26; 12:1, 5; 13:1; 14:23, 27; 15:3, 4, 22; 18:22; 20:17, 28). It is mentioned 54 more times in Romans through Revelation. Thus, the church is a major theme in Acts through Revelation. Nine of Paul's epistles were addressed to churches, three more to preachers, and the fourth to an individual who was a church leader. Hebrews, James, 1 & 2 Peter, 1 John, Jude, and Revelation were general epistles to the churches. Thus we see the major importance of the church to Christ and His apostles.

It is clear that the gospel was first spread into a diverse environment. Therefore, it is not surprising that the churches in the first century were also somewhat diverse. This was because when people were converted, they brought with them their own distinct world-views, national allegiances, customs, various philosophies, and remnants of their previous religious views (e.g., Jewish or pagan Greek/Roman). It is well-recognized that it takes time for a convert to relinquish man-made principles and teachings and to be converted completely to Christ and His teachings through the apostles. It is not easy to become the first-fruits of Christianity in a pagan, Jewish, or Islamic culture even today. Rejection by government, family, and friends is very painful, and murder because of faith in Christ is violently practiced by some even to this day.

Christ died the death of a martyr and became an example of such for all Christians. According to church history, all the apostles except John died the deaths of the martyrs. The murder of Stephen by the unbelieving Jews (Acts 7:54-60), Saul's widespread persecutions and murders of Christians (Acts 8; 22:4, 20; 26:9-11; 1 Corinthians 15:9; Galatians 1:13; Philippians 3:6; 1 Timothy 1:13), the murder of the apostle James by King Herod (Acts 12:2), the violent death of James, the half-brother of Jesus (Pamphilus, 1997, p. 2:23), and the subsequent murders of the apostles and other Christians by Nero and the following Roman Emperors until AD 313 claimed the lives of thousands upon thousands of Christians. Therefore, just dealing with the constant threat of murder by unbelievers took up significant emotional and intellectual resources of Christians in the first three centuries. Undoubtedly, this universal threat against Christianity established a certain degree of unity among Christians. The ancient proverb that says "The enemy of my enemy is my friend" is well-illustrated in the alliances of kings and kingdoms in the Old Testament. It also explains the sense of unity between diverse churches in the first three centuries.

The most obvious application of this ancient proverb in the New Testament was the presence of some degree of unity despite the apparent diversity between Jewish and Gentile churches. The first church that was established in Jerusalem was clearly Jewish in background, either by reason of being born a Jew or by reason of being a proselyte to Judaism (e.g., Nicolaus in Acts 6:5). Historically, the Jews did not associate, and especially did not eat with Gentiles. This made it impossible to evangelize the Gentiles after the Jerusalem church was established even though such an outreach was mandated by Christ's great commission (Matthew 28:18-20). However, approximately 10 years after the Jerusalem church was established, God took the initiative and chose the devout, God-fearing Gentile named Cornelius, a Roman centurion, and sent His angel to speak to Cornelius in a vision (Acts 10:1-8). At the same time God took the initiative and prepared Peter to open the kingdom to the Gentiles (Acts 10:9-33). Peter recognized God's hand in all this, and acknowledged this in his short sermon to Cornelius and his family (Acts 10:34-43). God again took the initiative and sent His Holy Spirit on these Gentiles and they spoke in tongues just as the apostles had done in Acts 2:1-4. The Jewish Christians with Peter were amazed that God had poured out His Holy Spirit "even on the Gentiles" (Acts 10:45). Because of God's actions, Peter immediately called for the baptisms of these Gentiles.

However, when Peter returned to Jerusalem, he was immediately confronted by the Jewish Christians:

> [1] Now the apostles and the brethren who were throughout Judea heard that the Gentiles also had received the word of God. [2] And when Peter came up to Jerusalem, those who were circumcised took issue with him, [3] saying, "You went to uncircumcised men and ate with them." Acts 11:1-3 (NASB)

Instead of being joyous that Christ's great commission had at last reached the Gentiles, these Jewish Christians were more concerned that Peter had gone to the Gentiles and had eaten with them. As people who continued to observe the Mosaic Law, they had reason to be concerned. God had repeatedly warned the ancient Israelites He had rescued from Egypt that they must utterly exterminate the Gentile pagans in the Promised Land, and by no means could they eat with these pagans as this would be participating in their idolatry (Exodus 34:11-16; Daniel 1:8-16). When they failed to drive out the Gentile pagans, the angel of the LORD confronted them in their disobedience and said that these idolatrous peoples "shall become thorns in your sides, and their gods shall be a snare to you" (Judges 2:3). Indeed, the Israelites repetitively fell into idolatry because they had not obeyed God in this matter. This same idolatry plagued both the Northern and Southern Kingdoms, and both went into foreign captivities because of it. Therefore, when the Jews came out of Babylonian captivity, they had a mind to abhor idolatry and abhor anything that might lead to idolatry, including eating with the idolatrous Gentile pagans. This explains the concerns of the Jewish Christians when they heard that Peter had eaten with them. However, Peter explained the whole matter to them successfully:

> [18] When they heard this, they quieted down and glorified God, saying, "Well then, God has granted to the Gentiles also the repentance that leads to life." Acts 11:18 (NASB)

Yet, this was not the end of the matter with the Gentiles who became Christians. As Paul preached and established congregations among the Gentiles, judaizing teachers from the Jerusalem church went to these Gentile churches and taught them that in addition to Christ, they had to be circumcised and follow the Law of Moses (Acts 15:1, 5). Therefore, Paul and Barnabas met with the apostles and elders of the Jerusalem church to discuss this matter (Acts 15:6-35). Peter's testimony was pointed:

> [7] After there had been much debate, Peter stood up and said to them, "Brethren, you know that in the early days God made a choice among you, that by my mouth the Gentiles would hear the word of the gospel and believe. [8] And God, who knows the heart, testified to them giving them the Holy Spirit, just as He also did to us; [9] and He made no distinction between us and them, cleansing their hearts by faith. [10] Now therefore why do you put God to the test by placing upon the neck of the disciples a yoke which neither our fathers nor we have been able to bear? [11] But we believe that we are saved through the grace of the Lord Jesus, in the same way as they also are." Acts 15:7-11 (NASB)

Peter understood from the conversion of Cornelius (Acts 10) that these Gentile Christians did not have to follow the Law of Moses, which Peter described as "a yoke which neither our fathers nor we have been able to bear." The conclusion drawn by those in the meeting agreed with Peter that the Gentile Christians did not have to follow the Mosaic Law. There were some issues that predated the Mosaic Law that the Gentiles needed to observe in order to have fellowship with Jewish Christians. These had to do with avoiding idolatry, sexual immorality, meat from strangled animals, and blood (Acts 15:19-20). The conclusion was put into the form of a letter, and this letter was sent to the Gentile churches in Antioch, Syria, and Cilicia.

However, like most meetings between people, this did not mean that the issue was resolved. Judaizing teachers continued in their zeal to enslave the Gentile churches by convincing them that they couldn't be saved unless they obeyed the Mosaic Law. Romans, Galatians, and Hebrews were written in part to argue this same issue. The conclusion continued to be that the Gentile Christians were not under the Mosaic Law; however, Paul went further than this in his writings and showed that the Jew had to die to the Law in order to be joined to Christ (Romans 7:1-6). Unfortunately, this was a message that the Jewish churches could not accept.

This issue highlighted a major difference between the Jewish Christian churches and the Gentile churches. Although the Jewish leadership had come to the conclusion that the Gentile churches didn't have to follow the Mosaic Law, the Jewish churches still felt obligated to follow it. This led to a Jerusalem church that, even after being in existence for approximately 27 years, was still zealous for and actively practicing the Mosaic Law. This is evident in the admonitions and requests James made to Paul in approximately AD 57, just before Paul was arrested:

> 17 After we arrived in Jerusalem, the brethren received us gladly.
> 18 And the following day Paul went in with us to James, and all
> the elders were present. 19 After he had greeted them, he began
> to relate one by one the things which God had done among the
> Gentiles through his ministry. 20 And when they heard it they be-
> gan glorifying God; and they said to him, "<u>You see, brother, how
> many thousands there are among the Jews of those who have be-
> lieved, and they are all zealous for the Law</u>; 21 and they have been
> told about you, that <u>you are teaching all the Jews who are among
> the Gentiles to forsake Moses, telling them not to circumcise their
> children nor to walk according to the customs</u>. 22 What, then, is to
> be done? They will certainly hear that you have come. 23 Therefore
> do this that we tell you. We have four men who are under a vow;
> 24 take them and purify yourself along with them, and pay their
> expenses so that they may shave their heads; and all will know

> that there is nothing to the things which they have been told about you, but that you yourself also walk orderly, keeping the Law. [25] But concerning the Gentiles who have believed, we wrote, having decided that they should abstain from meat sacrificed to idols and from blood and from what is strangled and from fornication." [26] Then Paul took the men, and the next day, purifying himself along with them, went into the temple giving notice of the completion of the days of purification, until the sacrifice was offered for each one of them. Acts 21:17-26 (NASB)

Note in James' comments above, that he admonished Paul and evidently believed Paul had gone beyond the agreement of Acts 15 and had taught Jewish Christians they didn't need to obey the Mosaic Covenant. There is reason to think James was accurate in his assessment that Paul was teaching Jews these things since neither Paul nor Peter lived as Jews in their evangelistic efforts among Gentiles (see Paul's teachings in Romans 7:1-6; 8:2; Galatians 2:19-21; 5:18; Ephesians 2:15; Colossians 2:14). The Jewish Christians still had the Temple in Jerusalem and the entirety of what it meant to be a Jew was deeply joined to this Temple. Evidently the Jewish Christians in Jerusalem had come to the conclusion that there had to be two different types of churches: one for the Jews, and one for the Gentiles. One church would observe the Mosaic Law, and the other church would not. The Jewish Christians could not accept living like or worshipping like the Gentile Christians. Thus, we find the first culturally-based division of the church. The Jewish leadership in the Jerusalem church even wanted Paul to compromise his teachings while he was in Jerusalem. Paul acquiesced and did what James had requested. However, James was wrong in his assessment of the situation and the desired outcome because Paul was nearly killed by the Jews when he was in the Temple and was arrested by the Romans at that time (Acts 21:27-36).

Many scholars today conclude from this data that we must have "unity in diversity." After all, if there was such a significant difference between the Jewish and Gentile churches and they were still thought to be one church, then there is no reason to not include everyone who believes in Christ as belonging to Christianity, regardless of their doctrines. However, is this justified? James was the half-brother of Jesus and was a prominent elder in the Jerusalem church. On the other hand, Paul was an apostle who was personally chosen and commissioned by Christ. Who had the greater authority? We know that Paul was inspired to write his many epistles, and these were from the very beginning acknowledged as being Scripture by both Peter and the churches. We also consider that James was inspired to write his epistle even though his was less well known and much less accepted by the early Christians. Eusebius considered James' epistle to be "disputed" (Pamphilus, 1997, p. 2:23). So who has the greater authority? Was it the apostle Paul or the elder James?

Before we eagerly jump to agree with the scholars, many of whom don't even believe in Christ's miraculous virgin birth or resurrection, and who also deny His miracles and the prophecies about Him—should we not pause here? If we take the side of the scholars, then we must conclude that Paul was mistaken in his teachings about the Law of Moses, as was the writer of Hebrews. These say we must die to the Law of Moses in order to be Christians. However, if we agree with the teachings of the apostle Paul, then we cannot agree with the scholars.

This was a difficult issue, even for Peter and Barnabas. Unfortunately, they were of a double mind. They certainly identified and ate with the Gentiles in Antioch. However, when Jewish Christians came from James in Jerusalem, Peter and Barnabas and the other Jews separated themselves from the Gentile Christians. Paul described this as follows:

> [11] But when Cephas came to Antioch, I opposed him to his face, because he stood condemned. [12] For prior to the coming of certain men from James, he used to eat with the Gentiles; but when they came, he began to withdraw and hold himself aloof, fearing the party of the circumcision. [13] The rest of the Jews joined him in hypocrisy, with the result that even Barnabas was carried away by their hypocrisy. [14] But when I saw that they were not straightforward about the truth of the gospel, I said to Cephas in the presence of all, "If you, being a Jew, live like the Gentiles and not like the Jews, how is it that you compel the Gentiles to live like Jews?" Galatians 2:11-14 (NASB)

Clearly, the apostle Paul rebuked the apostle Peter, Barnabas and the other Jews for their double-minded behavior. Paul was right in doing so because they had refused to admit before the delegation from James that the Gentiles had an equal benefit with the Jews in the great commission as Christ said they did (Matthew 28:18-20). So Paul was right.

It should be noted that Peter had realized that the Mosaic Law was not part of the New Covenant, and therefore he had no problem "living like Gentiles" when he was with the Gentiles. Paul did the same (1 Corinthians 9:19-23). However, Paul never backed down over what the Lord had revealed to him, regardless of whom he was with.

The future of the church in Jerusalem was short and filled with persecution from the Jews. Paul was arrested in AD 57, and James was martyred by his fellow Jews because of his faith in Christ in approximately AD 62. In AD 70 the Roman commander Titus came to make war on the Jews. He utterly destroyed Jerusalem along with hundreds of thousands of Jews. Fortunately the Jewish Christians, being informed by Christ's teaching (Matthew 24:15-22; Mark 13:14-20; Luke 19:41-44; 21:20-24) as well as revelation, left Jerusalem and went to Pella, which was one of the cities of the Decapolis in the Trans-Jordan area, as Eusebius later described:

> 3 But the people of the church in Jerusalem had been commanded by a revelation, vouchsafed to approved men there before the war, to leave the city and to dwell in a certain town of Perea called Pella. And when those that believed in Christ had come thither from Jerusalem, then, as if the royal city of the Jews and the whole land of Judea were entirely destitute of holy men, the judgment of God at length overtook those who had committed such outrages against Christ and his apostles, and totally destroyed that generation of impious men (Pamphilus, 1997, p. 3:5.3).

Therefore, from AD 70 onward, Jerusalem became a Gentile city, and Christianity became a Gentile movement.

Acts as a Restoration Pattern for Leadership of the Church

We discover very quickly in Acts God's pattern of leadership in the New Testament church. There were elders in the Jerusalem church (Acts

11:29-30; 15:2, 4, 6, 22, 23; 16:4; 21:18). At the close of their first missionary journey, Paul and Barnabas appointed elders in "every church" they had planted during that journey (Acts 14:23). Paul met with the elders from the Ephesians church and admonished them (Acts 20:17-38). This passage should be studied carefully by anyone who is contemplating becoming an elder, or anyone who is presently an elder. Here Paul tells these elders to

> [28] "Be on guard for yourselves and for all the flock, among which the Holy Spirit has made you overseers, to shepherd the church of God which He purchased with His own blood. Acts 20:28 (NASB)

Outside of Acts, we find more documentation of this biblical pattern of leadership. Titus was to appoint elders in each city of Crete (Titus 1:5-9) according to Paul's command. The elders were to pray for the sick of the congregation (James 5:14). Elders were to shepherd the church, exercising oversight in a willing manner, not for shameful gain, but eagerly, not domineering, but being examples (1 Peter 5:1-4). Members are to be in subjection to their elders (1 Peter 5:5). Elders are also called "overseers" (Titus 1:7; 1 Peter 2:25), and qualifications for this office are found in 1 Timothy 3:1-7. They are also called "shepherds" (Acts 20:28; 1 Peter 5:1-2), which gives an excellent description of the practical work of an elder.

Paul gives an overview of the leadership God gave for the church, and He also specified what that leadership is expected to accomplish. This is found in Ephesians 4:11-16.

> [11] And He gave some as <u>apostles</u>, and some as <u>prophets</u>, and some as <u>evangelists</u>, and some as <u>pastors and teachers</u>, [12] for the equipping of the saints for the work of service, to the building up of the body of Christ; [13] until we all attain to the unity of the faith, and of the knowledge of the Son of God, to a mature man, to the measure of the stature which belongs to the fullness of Christ. [14] As a result, we are no longer to be children, tossed here and there by waves and carried about by every wind of doctrine, by the trickery of men, by craftiness in deceitful scheming; [15] but speaking the truth in love, we are to grow up in all aspects into Him who is the

> head, even Christ, [16] from whom the whole body, being fitted and held together by what every joint supplies, according to the proper working of each individual part, causes the growth of the body for the building up of itself in love. Ephesians 4:11-16 (NASB)

The **apostles** are the original 12 apostles and Matthias who replaced Judas. We also know of Christ's special selection of Paul. With the exception of Judas, all the apostles died with no successors. However, we have the writings of the apostles today in the New Testament. We must follow their commands today just as we follow Christ's commands.

The **prophets** were men who received their message directly from God and spoke that message to the people. Agabus is a good example of a New Testament prophet (Acts 11:28; 21:10). As with the apostles, the miraculous manifestations of the Holy Spirit in prophecy have passed away (1 Corinthians 13:8-9). However we have, in the New Testament, prophets including the inspired Mark, Luke, James, and Jude. We can read from these prophets everyday to gain instruction and wisdom.

The **evangelists** were plentiful, and Paul wrote epistles to Timothy and Titus who were evangelists. An evangelist could be someone ministering to one church like Timothy when he was at Ephesus, or one ministering to several congregations and had to travel much in order to accomplish this. Examples of this are Titus on the island of Crete, and also Philip the evangelist in Samaria and Caesarea (Acts 8; 21:8). We have living evangelists today, and they are very important. They are the ones who proclaim the gospel. They must teach sound doctrine. One who is an evangelist must read 1 & 2 Timothy and Titus so he will be constantly reminded about what an evangelist must do. Evangelists in New Testament times became such by following one of the apostles or other seasoned leaders in their daily work. This type of "education" was like Christ's education of His apostles.

The **pastors and teachers** are both from the same group in the Greek. In this passage, the Greek word for "pastor" is ποιμήν (poimēn), and this word is uniformly translated as "shepherd" in the English Bibles all 18 times it appears in the New Testament, except for this passage where it is often translated "pastor." As demonstrated in the English Standard Version of the Bible, there is no reason to change the translation to "pastor" here in Ephesians 4:11 since it refers to the shepherds of the congregation, i.e., the elders or overseers. Specifically, these are shepherds who also teach the flock.

Ephesians 4:12-16 gives an excellent description of what must be accomplished by this four-fold leadership. If we choose to not have an evangelist, not have elders, or deny the authority of the written apostles and prophets, then we have turned our backs on the only God-given description of New Testament church leadership. We cannot be the New Testament church if we are not trying to have the New Testament leadership it mandates.

Acts as a Restoration Pattern for Church Autonomy

Another aspect of New Testament leadership is that each local church has its own leadership. This means that each church in the first century was "autonomous." The word "autonomous" is not found in the Bible; however, it was coined to describe a phenomenon found in the New Testament. The word does not mean that we are independent of Christ and His apostles for that would mean total apostasy. Rather, the term "autonomous" means that in issues of Christian freedom, that is, where God has not given a command, the local church is self-ruling. For example, we must meet each first day of the week, but God didn't tell us what time we must meet. So if one church meets at 8 AM and another church meets at 9 AM, there is no problem because each church can have its own policy in matters of Christian freedom. However, no one is free to preach some other gospel or to make up his own doctrine.

The defense for church autonomy rests on three major arguments (Anonymous, The Autonomy of the Local Church, 2010). These are as follows:

1. The first is based upon elderships in the first century. Each church in the first century had its own elders (Acts 14:23). These elders were to "shepherd the flock of God among you" (1 Peter 5:1-5). This means that each church was autonomous in leadership.
2. The second is based on the church treasury. Each individual church treasury was autonomous from all other churches' treasuries. This is seen in Acts 5:3-4 where Ananias' contribution

remained in his control until he gave it to the church. Further, no one could command a church to give to a certain cause without the church agreeing. New Testament churches were not taxed by some central religious organization.

3. The third is based on the interpretation of Acts 15. The meeting described in Acts 15 was not a "church counsel" and so this meeting did not violate congregational autonomy. Rather it was leadership from two churches (Jerusalem and Antioch) who met to discuss an issue that was between them (Ferguson, 1996, p. 345). This kind of meeting could not be held today because we have no living apostles that could provide the inspired counsel that solved the problem.

Therefore, in matters of opinion, expediency and human judgment, the local churches are "autonomous" and "self-governing." However, church autonomy must not lead to isolation. In the early church there was cooperation, mutual assistance, and communication. There was a sense of being one body in the Lord. Churches demonstrated mutual cooperation in the first century (Acts 11:28-30; Romans 15:25-26; 2 Corinthians 8:1-5) (Ferguson, 1996, p. 345).

REFLECTIONS

In conclusion, the book of Acts gives us much insight into what we must do to be saved. Because this pattern is from Christ, we must not change it. Rather, we should faithfully follow it. In addition, Acts gives us essential information regarding the church. In the case of the judaizing teachers, we learn that if the church leaves its apostolic foundation, then it will advocate teachings that are not in the New Covenant. This leads to confusion and division. In addition, Acts informs us of what kind of church government God has ordained. Each church should have its own elders. Each church should understand the four-fold leadership that God had ordained and persistently seek to establish that leadership. Leaders and committees should be replaced by elders and deacons in every congregation.

As those first century churches followed these apostolic teachings, they were restoring that New Covenant in their own day. In the same way, as we see these things and do them, we will be restoring the New Covenant in our own day.

When we sit down to read the New Testament today, it is essential that we understand it as it was first written. We must not add to the New Testament or take away from it. We must not "twist" the Scriptures to our own liking. Rather, we should be convicted and changed by God's Word.

Now as we move on to the epistles, we also find that they are witnesses to the continuing need for restoration of the New Covenant among the churches of the first century AD. Even a cursory view of the epistles shows that most of them were written in response to problems in the church. In all of these settings the epistles were written to correct and restore the New Covenant among those believers. Just as there were several good kings in Judah who restored the Mosaic Covenant, so also each New Testament epistle was restoring the New Covenant in that day. Therefore, we will explore the Pauline Epistles to find evidence of the New Covenant as God wanted it.

Study Questions

1. Do the Gospels show that Christ sent the apostles to preach the gospel, stressing Christ's death and resurrection, leading people to repent and become disciples of Christ, confessing Christ as the Son of God, baptizing them and teaching them to obey all the Christ has commanded?
2. Must we obey the apostles as well as Christ?
3. Are there many examples of conversions in the book of Acts that illustrate what is required to become a biblical Christian?
4. In regard to the outreach of the church to include the Gentiles, was this initiated by God or by men? Was it commanded by Christ? Where?
5. Were there differences between the Jewish Christians in Jerusalem and the Gentile Christians scattered all over the Roman Empire?

6. In what year was Jerusalem and the Temple destroyed in fulfillment of Christ's prophecy?
7. Did Paul and Barnabas appoint elders in every church they planted on their first missionary journey?
8. Did Paul command Titus to appoint elders in every church they planted on the Island of Crete?
9. What does church autonomy mean? Is this term found in the Bible?
10. If a church says it is autonomous, does that mean they are allowed to violate the teachings of Christ or His apostles?
11. Is church autonomy only applicable to matters of opinion, and not applicable to Christ's or the apostles' commands, approved examples, or necessary inferences?

Chapter 9

New Covenant—Romans to Ephesians

The Pauline Epistles as Restoration Documents

The Pauline epistles will be presented in a summary fashion in order to illustrate how we should view them as restoration documents. At this point I have not completed my presentation of the remaining New Testament documents to illustrate that they are also restoration documents. However, after my reading of these Scriptures for decades, I feel confident that they too will show the same attributes.

I especially have chosen the Pauline epistles because historically they were suppressed in second century AD and thereafter. This suppression allowed the onslaught of multiple digressions from the Scriptural mandates regarding the church in the Pauline epistles. The reformers in the 1500's rediscovered Paul's writings and that rediscovery fueled the Reformation in Europe. In a similar fashion, the Restoration Movement in the USA starting in the 1800's was also fueled by the Pauline epistles. Currently, liberal theologians are striving to convince Christians that the Pauline epistles are nothing more than "love letters to the churches," thereby denying their applicability for Christianity today. This represents a new suppression of the Pauline epistles so that the liberal theologians can achieve their own agenda regarding the church, that is, to free Christianity from the commands of the

Apostle Paul. Thus, it is appropriate for us to reconsider the writings of the Christ-appointed, Christ-commissioned, and Christ-inspired Apostle Paul as we study these principles of God's Covenants and Restorations.

Romans

The book of Romans is the longest of Paul's letters. It was written approximately AD 57 from Corinth. The purpose of this letter was to present a full exposition of the gospel as well as defend Paul's mission to the Gentiles. Paul's thesis was,

> [16] For I am not ashamed of the gospel, for it is the power of God for salvation to everyone who believes, to the Jew first and also to the Greek. [17] For in it the righteousness of God is revealed from faith to faith; as it is written, "BUT THE RIGHTEOUS man SHALL LIVE BY FAITH." Romans 1:16-17 (NASB)

- Romans 1:1-17—Paul's introduction and theme.
- Romans 1:18 to 3:20—All people, including all Jews and Gentiles, are under condemnation and need the righteousness that comes from God.
- Romans 3:21 to 4:25—Righteousness is only achieved by faith in Christ, and cannot be obtained by keeping the Law.
- Romans 5:1 to 8:39—The implications of being justified by faith.
- Romans 9:1 to 11:36—The reason God made a sovereign choice and rejected of Israel.
- Romans 12:1 to 15:13—Because of God's grace, we are obligated to live a devoted life.
- Romans 15:14 to 16:27—Paul's concluding remarks, warnings, and farewell.

REFLECTIONS

Paul's Epistle to the Romans is a wonderful book. There is so much hope and assurance from God in this epistle. First we see the Gentiles and the Jews—all of us as lost without Christ. We see the strong apostolic delivery of the doctrine of justification by faith in Christ and apart from the works of the Mosaic Law. We see God's love and blessing poured out on us in Christ. In response to this incredible deliverance, love, and grace of God, we respond by not letting sin reign in us and by presenting our bodies to God as instruments of righteousness, for we are slaves to righteousness and not slaves to sin. We remember that our baptism taught us to die to sin. We understand that the Jews were released from the Law. This is good because the Law cannot give life, but only death. But we are alive with Christ and fellow heirs with Him. The Spirit helps us, and God's love surrounds us. We understand what happened to the Jews, and hope they will repent and believe in Christ that they may be restored to God. We are to be living sacrifices with the marks of being true Christians. We must submit to our governmental authorities. We will fulfill the Law through love. We will not judge each other regarding matters of opinions. Rather, we will seek that none should stumble. We will follow the example of the humble Christ. We will also try to fulfill the Great Commission just as the zealous apostle Paul did with all his might. Yes, Paul's Epistle to the Romans gives us much to restore.

1 Corinthians

The book of 1 Corinthians was written to correct immoral practices and doctrinal errors in this congregation. The letter was written in AD 57 from Ephesus.

- 1 Corinthians 1:1 to 4:21—There were divisions in the church.
- 1 Corinthians 5:1 to 6:20—Flee sexual immorality; stop lawsuits against believer.
- 1 Corinthians 7:1-40—There were problems regarding marriage, divorce, and remarriage.
- 1 Corinthians 8:1 to 11:1—Flee idolatry.
- 1 Corinthians 11:2-16—Use head coverings for women in the church.
- 1 Corinthians 11: 17-34—Observe the Lord's Supper in a proper manner.

- 1 Corinthians 12:1 to 14:25—Use miraculous spiritual gifts properly and recognize the supremacy of love.
- 1 Corinthians 14:26-39—Conduct orderly worship.
- 1 Corinthians 15:1-58—Paul defends the resurrection.
- 1 Corinthians 16:1-4—Collections to be made for the Saints.
- 1 Corinthians 16:5-24—Paul writes closing personal matters and greetings.

REFLECTIONS

Therefore, what can we learn about restoring the New Testament church from the Corinthians? Surely it was one of the most troubled churches in the New Testament. However, we learn much about what a church should be from the remarks of the Apostle Paul which were given to the Corinthian church for correction. We must glorify Christ and not allow ourselves to be split into factions or cliques. We must not go beyond what is written (1 Corinthians 4:6). We must not tolerate sexual immorality in the church, and we must avoid sexual immorality in our own lives like we would flee from the plague. We must understand God's principles for marriage, including one man with one woman until death separates us, and we must abhor divorce. We must flee idolatry and never allow anything in our lives to be more important than God, for that is the essence of idolatry. Each church needs to support its own preacher. We must understand the biblical role of women in the church. We must use their talents for the glory of Christ, but we must never put them into situations that are forbidden by God. We must learn that love is eternal and greater than any of the miraculous gifts of the Holy Spirit. We must always have an orderly worship. We must never lose our faith in the resurrection of Christ. We must give back to God from that which He had given us. If we observe these things, we will be restoring the New Covenant and the New Testament church.

2 Corinthians

The book of 2 Corinthians was written in approximately AD 57 from somewhere in Macedonia. Of all Paul's epistles, it is the least systematic and the most personal.

- 2 Corinthians 1:1 to 7:16—The apostle Paul presents a defense of his life and work.
- 2 Corinthians 8:1 to 9:15—Paul gives instructions regarding the collections for the poor saints in Jerusalem and provides principles for giving.
- 2 Corinthians 10:1 to 13:14—Paul defends his apostleship.

REFLECTIONS

There are some important lessons we need to learn from 2 Corinthians. This church still had significant spiritual problems even after Paul had written his first epistle to the Corinthians and had visited them twice. Yet, Paul still loved them greatly despite their failings. This is perhaps the most important lesson for us today: Paul didn't give up on churches just because they had significant doctrinal problems. On the other hand, Paul was not at all embarrassed to speak clearly, nor was he hesitant to rebuke the sins and exhort them to better behavior. This also we must learn. It is not love to overlook doctrinal error. However, Paul was clearly diplomatic: he always communicated love with a self-effacing and humble manner in the midst of judgment. Only when he was backed against the wall regarding his apostleship did the apostle outline his experiences of severe persecution.

A man had been disfellowshipped (1 Corinthians 5), but he had repented and Paul then instructed the church to forgive him. However, they were not only to forgive, but comfort and reaffirm their love for him. When a Christian confesses before the church his/her sin and asks for forgiveness, he/she is very vulnerable. In many instances in America, that event is so traumatic that often the one who confesses will never return to church again. Because of this, people are reluctant to confess their sins before the church. We must learn how to be supportive of people who repent.

We must also understand that we are not under the Mosaic Law but under the New Covenant which is mediated by Christ. Let us not fall back into that Old Covenant for as Gentiles that Old Covenant was never given to us. We cannot earn our way to heaven by doing the commandments of the Mosaic Covenant. Also, let us not fall into a legalistic mentality regarding the New Covenant in which justification, sanctification, and salvation are based on our works and not God's grace.

Paul was a minster of that New Covenant. We need to join him in that venture, if for no other purpose than knowing the fear of the Lord (2 Corinthians 5:11). We need to be a part of that ministry of reconciliation, imploring people to be reconciled to God and pointing to the atoning death of Christ on the cross as the means of that reconciliation.

We must be holy. That is mocked in the world today. However, God does not mock holiness in us. We must separate ourselves from sin and live for God. When there is sin in our lives, we must repent.

Paul gives us many principles concerning giving back to the Lord. We should learn these and use them. We need to learn how to grow in our giving. We are not under the tithe, but it is disgraceful how so many Christians give God next to nothing. Should we be giving less than the Jews because God has given us more spiritual blessings than the Jews ever knew?

We need to honor the apostles of Christ. To criticize and undermine the apostles' authority or to disobey their commands is dangerous. They speak for Christ. The apostles were hand-picked and commissioned by Christ. Christ spoke through them. The signs of a true apostle were evident: signs, wonders, and mighty works (2 Corinthians 12:12). Can it ever be good in the final judgment to have ignored the apostles' teachings?

If we keep such thoughts in our minds and do them, then we will be restoring the New Covenant.

Galatians

The book of Galatians was written in AD 48 to the churches of provincial territory of South Galatia, which would include the churches in Antioch of Pisidia, Iconium, Lystra, and Derbe. Paul planted all these churches during his 1 missionary journey (AD 46-47). The occasion for this letter was that Judaizing teachers had taught these congregations that they could not be saved unless they followed the Law of Moses and were circumcised. Paul's theme is as follows:

> [16] ...nevertheless knowing that a man is not justified by the works of the Law but through faith in Christ Jesus, even we have believed in Christ Jesus, so that we may be justified by faith in Christ and not by the works of the Law; since by the works of the Law no flesh will be justified. Galatians 2:16 (NASB)

- Galatians 1:1 to 2:21—Paul defends his apostolic authority. He reveals that anyone who adds to or takes away from the gospel will be accursed. The Judaizing teachers had added to the gospel by requiring obedience to the Law of Moses and circumcision as necessary for salvation. Therefore, Christianity must exclude all other teachings from the New Covenant.
- Galatians 3:1 to 4:31—Seven arguments that show the superiority of faith over law (the Holy Spirit, Abraham, the curse of the Old Testament law, a human will, the child keeper, Paul's personal plea, and the allegory of Hagar and Sarah).
- Galatians 5:1 to 6:18—The gospel of grace leads to true freedom and godly living.

REFLECTIONS

The message of Galatians begins with the gospel and the way the Galatians had made it into "another gospel" by adding the Mosaic Law to it. We must not add to or take away from the gospel for if we do, we will be accursed and condemned by God.

We are again confronted with the apostleship of Paul. There are so many who call themselves Christians but who reject the Christ-given teachings through Paul. Paul had to struggle for his apostleship while alive because the Judaizing teachers would never let anyone forget that Paul had persecuted the church before his conversion. Many false prophets tried to capitalize on any seeming weakness in Paul so they could exalt themselves over Paul. The same is true even today. However, Christ called and commissioned Paul to be one of His apostles. There is no other explanation for his conversion and his miracles. Paul was a genuine Christ-appointed apostle.

Paul teaches without apology that we are justified by faith and not by works of the Mosaic Law (Galatians 2:16; 3:24). He teaches this same doctrine in his epistle to the Romans (Romans 3:28; 4:1-5; 5:1). Paul also teaches that this justification is by God's grace (Romans 3:24), and we gain access into that grace by faith (Romans 5:2). Furthermore, Luke, and by implication Paul, teaches that even our faith is by God's grace (Acts 16:14; 18:27). Jesus said to the sinful woman who anointed his head and kissed his feet that her sins were forgiven and "Your faith has saved you" (Luke 7:48-50). Paul gives a stunning summary of this concept of grace, faith and salvation:

> [4] But God, being rich in mercy, because of His great love with which He loved us, [5] even when we were dead in our transgressions, made us alive together with Christ (by grace you have been saved), [6] and raised us up with Him, and seated us with Him in the heavenly places in Christ Jesus, [7] so that in the ages to come He might show the surpassing riches of His grace in kindness toward us in Christ Jesus. [8] For by grace you have been saved through faith; and that not of yourselves, it is the gift of God; [9] not as a result of works, so that no one may boast. [10] For we are His workmanship, created in Christ Jesus for good works, which God prepared beforehand so that we would walk in them. Ephesians 2:4-10 (NASB)

Brothers and sisters, these teachings on God's grace, our faith and our salvation tend to be minimized among some of us. It appears to be threatening to some Christians. However, without embracing these doctrines, we will not have peace and reassurance in our souls. If we don't make these teachings our own, we will continue to have members who are uncertain of their salvation. Indeed, they say they are not sure they are saved because they are uncertain if they have done more good than bad. Comments such as this reveal a "works salvation" rather than a salvation based on grace. Often those in the USA who minimize these writings from Paul will frequently rebaptize because they are not sure they are really saved. I realize that we have tended to minimize these Scriptures because of those who would go beyond these Scriptures, saying that they are saved by faith ONLY, saying that they can NEVER fall from grace, saying that ANY sort of baptism at any age is fine since we are saved by grace or saying that repentance is NOT NECESSARY—all because they are saved by grace. However, we must never allow those who preach false doctrine to define what we preach or believe as Christians. We must not be embarrassed by what Paul wrote on this subject or leave it out of our instructions for the church. This teaching is central to what we must believe about salvation.

Paul believed in a working faith (see above in Ephesians 2:10). James said that faith without works is dead (James 2:14-17). The writer of Hebrews wrote, "By faith" numerous times to describe the faith of the biblical heroes. If our faith does not move us to repent of our sins, confess our faith in Christ as Lord, and be baptized for the remission of sins and to receive the gift of the Holy Spirit, then we don't have that one and only biblical apostolic faith. If our faith doesn't move us to obey all that Christ commanded (Matthew 28:20) and obey all the apostolic teachings, then we do not have that one and only biblical apostolic faith.

Therefore, all these things Paul says about God's grace, our faith, and our salvation are true. In addition, it is also true that we must obey God's commands because faith without works is dead. Faith is what launches us on our Christian journey, and it is what establishes the beginning of our covenant with God. But we must continue our walk because our faith is proved by our actions, yes, by our obedience to God. For just as Abraham believed God and God counted it to him as righteousness (Genesis 15:6), so also Abraham had to demonstrate his faith by obeying God's commands regarding circumcision (Genesis 17:10-14) and the sacrifice of Isaac his son (Genesis 22:1-19). For God said these things about Abraham when He stopped him from sacrificing Isaac:

> [10] Abraham stretched out his hand and took the knife to slay his son. [11] But the angel of the LORD called to him from heaven and said, "Abraham, Abraham!" And he said, "Here I am." [12] He said, "Do not stretch out your hand against the lad, and do nothing to him; for <u>now I know that you fear God, since you have not</u>

> withheld your son, your only son, from Me." Genesis 22:10-12 (NASB)

Had Abraham not complied with God's commands, he would have broken the covenant with God. But Abraham did not disobey. Rather, this is what God said to Isaac about his father Abraham, the man whom God had justified by faith:

> [4] "I will multiply your descendants as the stars of heaven, and will give your descendants all these lands; and by your descendants all the nations of the earth shall be blessed; [5] because Abraham obeyed Me and kept My charge, My commandments, My statutes and My laws." Genesis 26:4-5 (NASB)

Therefore, let us vigorously defend the New Testament doctrine that we were saved by grace through faith. And let us also vigorously defend the New Testament doctrine that we must obey God. These two doctrines do not contradict or exclude each other if we understand them well. If this is not true, then how could Paul champion salvation by grace through faith and at the same time tell us of sins, which, if we do them, we will "not inherit the kingdom of God" (Galatians 5:19-21)?

Let us then be like Abraham, the father of faith and of the faithful (Romans 4:11-12). However, let us not be like the sons of Israel, for they were faithless. Yes, they were the descendents of Abraham. They even saw the mighty works, wonders and signs that God brought upon Pharaoh and all the Egyptians as well as the utter humiliation and defeat God brought on the Egyptian idols with His 10 plagues, yet these things did not move them to worship only God. They saw that they were chosen because of their righteous forefathers Abraham, Isaac, and Jacob, but they themselves did not try to imitate the faith of their fathers. Could they not see that God was saving them by His grace and not by their works? Did He not lead them through the Red Sea and yet totally destroy Pharaoh and his chariots in the Red Sea? That divine act was not based on their works because they showed no faith at the Red Sea and even cried out that they should return to Egypt (Exodus 14:10-12). They grumbled against Moses because of the bitter waters at Marah (Exodus 15:24). They wished that they had died at the hands of the Egyptians because they missed the meat pots they had in Egypt (Exodus 16:2-3). They refused to obey the Sabbath (Exodus 16:27-28). They demanded water to drink at Rephidim instead of humbly asking God (Exodus 17:1-4). All of this was before they reached Mt. Sinai and received the Mosaic Covenant. Yet, when Moses went up on the mountain to receive the Lord's commandments, the Israelites again showed their idolatry by making an idol and doing terrible acts of idolatry instead of worshiping God Almighty and giving Him thanks for his mercies and deliverance (Deuteronomy 9). It appears that it was at this time that God said,

> [4] 'You are to perform My judgments and keep My statutes, to live in accord with them; I am the LORD your God. [5] 'So you shall keep My statutes and My judgments, by which a man may live if he does them; I am the LORD.' Leviticus 18:4-5 (NASB)

They refused to accept salvation by grace through faith because of their little faith. Therefore, God gave them the curse of the Law (Galatians 3:12-13) as quoted above. To crown their unbelief and rebellion against God, they refused to go into the Promised Land and conquer it (Numbers 14:1-10). Their forty years in the wilderness, the sentence for their unbelief and rebellion, was marked by their stubbornness, and this characterized Israelite history for the next 1500 years, including their rejection of the Messiah in the New Testament.

Therefore, let us not be legalists and act and speak as if we have saved ourselves by our own acts of righteousness. This will be like living under the curse of the Old Law just as the Jews did. Truly, such thoughts will be filled with emptiness and end in smothering doubt. Rather, let us embrace salvation by grace through faith in Christ because that is what the New Testament teaches. Then let us show a faith that works, that is, a working faith that displays the biblical marks of obedience. Yet our trust must remain in God and not our acts. Our acts of obedience to God are frequently performed in weakness because we are humans. Therefore, let us rely on God and not ourselves. Let us never insult Him by claiming we have saved ourselves by the strength of our own virtuous determinations and by the pristine holiness of our own righteous acts.

Ephesians

The book of Ephesians was written in approximately AD 62 during Paul's first imprisonment at Rome. It appears to be a circular letter to the churches in Asia Minor. The reasons for this include the absence of personal greetings, problematic doctrines, or unchristian behaviors. Paul's other letters to churches were generally written in the midst of a controversy of some kind. However, this does not appear to be the case with his letter to the Ephesians.

- Ephesians 1:1-23—Paul writes a salutation and recalls the blessings in Christ. Christ is head over all things for the church, which is his body, the fullness of him who fills all in all.
- Ephesians 2:1-22—Paul reveals God's salvation by grace through faith for both Jews and Gentiles. The law of commandments and ordinances were abolished so there could be unity in the church.
- Ephesians 3:1-21—The mystery of the gospel is revealed: the Gentiles are fellow heirs in Christ through the gospel. This revealed mystery is proclaimed through the church to all those in the heavenly places by the eternal purpose of God. There is eternal glory for God in the church and in Christ Jesus.
- Ephesians 4:1 to 6:24—Paul defines the Christian's response to God's salvation. We must keep the unity of the Spirit in the bond of peace. Paul reveals the seven-fold basis for unity. The new life is defined by holiness and the avoidance of sin. We must imitate God by walking in love. We must walk in the light and in wisdom. We must display Christian principles in relationships (wives and husbands, children and parents, slaves and masters). The relationship of Christ to the church is repeatedly compared to the marriage relationship. Paul reveals our spiritual enemies as well as our armor from God.

REFLECTIONS

This is an extremely important epistle. It addresses what we must believe in order to be Christians and what kind of lives we must live.

Christians and the church have always been in the plan of God, even before the beginning of time. Therefore, the church was not some afterthought of God as some claim. Indeed, the church is exalted throughout the epistle, and this shows the importance of the church to God. The church revealed by Christ through His apostles should also be very important to us. Salvation is found only in Jesus Christ and it is obtained by grace through faith. Paul brings to our remembrance how lost we Gentiles are without Christ. God took the first step to save us in Christ. He abolished the Mosaic Law so there could be peace and unity in the church. God established the church on the apostles and prophets, with Christ as the cornerstone. Paul reveals the meaning of the mystery of the gospel, and the mystery is that the Gentiles in Christ are fellow heirs with Jews in salvation.

Now concerning Paul's applications to these teachings, he shows the prerequisites to unity, and then the platform for unity in his series of 7 singularities. We must never compromise these because God never compromised these. The one church is again exalted as well as the one Spirit, one hope, the one way we are converted (one Lord, one faith, one baptism) as well as the Fatherhood of God, which is the universal call to unity. Brothers and sisters, all denominational calls for unity deny many of these essentials. Therefore, we cannot have unity with them. Paul then speaks of the God-given leadership for the church and what that leadership must accomplish. Paul then speaks of the new life in Christ and enumerates many virtues we must practice and vices we must abandon. He then specifically comments on relationships between wives and husbands, children and parents, and slaves and masters. In these Paul shows what "submitting to one another out of reverence for Christ" means. Those who appear to be "stronger" in these relationships have the greater burden of responsibility to love, teach and be humble. Those who appear to be "weaker" in these relationships must demonstrate submission. Paul closes by speaking about the "armor of God," and this armor is essential to every Christian in every age.

If we restore the teachings of Ephesians, we will be restoring the New Covenant.

Study Questions

1. Why were Paul's epistles suppressed in the 2 Century AD and thereafter?
2. What movement in Europe starting in the 1500's was fueled by Paul's epistles?
3. What movement in America starting in the 1800's was fueled by Paul's epistles?
4. Why are liberal theologians leading a movement now to suppress the authority of Paul's epistles? How should we respond to restore the Christ-inspired Pauline epistles today?
5. Does Paul teach the doctrine of justification, sanctification, and salvation by God's grace through faith in Christ? Are we ashamed of this teaching? How can we embrace this teaching without rejecting the authority of the Bible?
6. Does Paul teach that since we are justified by grace through faith, we don't have to obey God anymore, or we can choose what we will and won't obey?

Chapter 10

New Covenant—Philippians to 2 Thessalonians

The Pauline Epistles as Restoration Documents

Philippians

The book of Philippians was written in approximately AD 63 during Paul's first imprisonment at Rome. Paul writes to the Christians at Philippi to thank them for the gift they sent to him. It is a very warm and loving letter, and he shares with them his own circumstances. However, Paul also appears to be concerned about unity in this church (Philippians 2:1-11; 4:2-3) as well as the presence of Judaizing teachers (Philippians 3:2, 18).

- Philippians 1:1-11—Paul writes his salutation, thanksgiving and prayer.
- Philippians 1:12-26—Paul speaks of the advance of the gospel. Paul writes of those who preach from perverse motives in order to make his imprisonment more painful, but Paul rejoices that Christ is preached. For Paul, "to live is Christ, and to die is gain."
- Philippians 1:27 to 2:18—We must imitate Christ's humility. We must obey God and work out our own salvation with fear

and trembling, knowing that God works in us for His good pleasure. We must become blameless, innocent, and without blemish.

- Philippians 2:19-30—Paul writes about his helpers, Timothy and Epaphroditus.
- Philippians 3:1-16—Paul warns of the Judaizing teachers. He reminds them of his own radical repentance, turning from a false confidence in the Law to a righteousness that depends on faith in Christ. Paul suffered enormous losses, but gained Christ. Paul yearns to know Christ and the power of His resurrection, to share His sufferings, becoming like Him in His death that he might also attain to the resurrection of the dead. Paul presses on, forgetting what lies behind and straining forward to what lies ahead, even Christ. This is mature thinking, and without it we cannot escape our own failings.
- Philippians 3:17-21—Paul commands the Christians to imitate him and other mature Christians. He warns about the enemies of the cross of Christ. Our citizenship must be in heaven, and we must wait patiently for our Savior. We will be transformed to be like Him who is all-powerful when He returns.
- Philippians 4:1-9—Paul now exhorts us to stand firm, to seek unity in the church, to rejoice in Christ, to be reasonable, and to pray without anxiety. He promises the peace of God which will guard our hearts and minds in Christ. We must think about what is honorable, just, pure, lovely, commendable, excellent, and worthy. Paul commands us to imitate him.
- Philippians 4:10-20—Paul thanks them for their generous gift, and calls it a fragrant offering, a sacrifice acceptable and pleasing to God. He knows that God will help them in every need.
- Philippians 4:21-23—Paul sends his final greetings.

REFLECTIONS

Paul encouraged the Philippians to imitate Christ's example of humility (Philippians 2:1-11). This is very important in the setting of the church because this humility will maintain unity in the church. Paul also encouraged the Philippians to imitate his own example of being a Christian (Philippians 3:17; 4: 9). Paul encouraged the Corinthians to do the same (1 Corinthians 4:6), and the specific issue there was to learn by his example "not to go beyond what is written." When we imitate Christ and the apostles, we are admitting that there is a New Testament pattern that we must restore in our own times.

Paul spends much time in this epistle, just as he does in almost all of his epistles, in defining the Christian life. He does so by using both positives attributes (what we must become) and negative attributes (what we must abandon). These virtues and vices greatly help to define how we as Christians must live today. This kind of careful instruction was continued through the first 500 years of Christianity, and was known as the "Two Ways." It is found in several Christian writings from the first to the fifth centuries. These sources include the following:

1. *The Didache*
2. *The Epistle of Barnabas*
3. *The Didascalia*
4. *The Apostolic Church Order*
5. *The Summary of Doctrine*
6. *The Apostolic Constitutions*
7. *The Life of Shenoute*
8. *On the Teachings of the Apostles (or Doctrina Apostolorum) (Holmes, 1992, 1999, 2007, pp. 335-336)*

One way led to life, and the other way led to death. One way led to heaven, and the other way led to hell. We need to recognize this type of apostolic training and also work hard to define biblically the Christian life today using the same values as the apostles used.

As with other epistles of Paul, he once again reaffirms the "righteousness from God that depends on faith" (Philippians 3:9). If Paul could not be saved by his meritorious works, neither can we.

We should also have the missionary mind of the Philippian church. They partnered with Paul in a special and lasting ministry. God will certainly reward them for their "fragrant offering, a sacrifice acceptable and pleasing to God." He will also reward us if we do as the Philippian church did.

Therefore, the church of today has much to restore from Paul's epistle to the Philippians. But if we do so, we will be restoring the New Covenant.

Colossians

The book of Colossians was written in approximately A.D. 60 to counteract false teachers. The major problem confronting the church in Colossae was Gnosticism. This was characterized by philosophy, empty deceit and human traditions, but was not according to Christ (Colossians 2:8). There were also elements in this false doctrine regarding food, drink, festivals, new moons, and Sabbaths, all of which suggest a Jewish influence (Colossians 2:16). There were also sensuous elements of asceticism, worship of angels, and visions (Colossians 2:18). This false doctrine was being preached by certain false teachers. To counter this, Paul preached the preeminence of Christ in all things, including Him as head of the body, which is the church (Colossians 1:15-20), and the filling of Christians with Christ (Colossians 2:10) and not with man-made wisdom or philosophy.

- Colossians 1:1-14—Paul offers his salutation, thanksgiving and prayer for the Colossians, emphasizing the need for the knowledge of God as well as spiritual wisdom and understanding.
- Colossians 1:15-20—Paul extols Christ as being preeminent in all things and as the head of the church, which is His body. Christ is the Creator, and Christ holds the cosmos together. Christ is the first in rank of those who will be resurrected. God reconciles everything to Himself through Christ, making peace by the blood of His cross.
- Colossians 1:21-23—Paul applies this preeminence of Christ to the Colossians in their conversions. Christ has reconciled them and presented them as holy, blameless and without reproach to God—however, this standing is conditional on their steadfast faith in Christ.
- Colossians 1:24 to 2:5—Paul reminds them of his ministry to the churches. He warns them not to be deceived with plausible argu-

ments that would weaken their faith in God, and would transfer their trust to the wisdom of men.

- Colossians 2:6-15—Paul contrasts the false man-made doctrine with all that the preeminent Christ has done for the Colossians. Since they received Christ, they must walk in Him. They were filled by Christ when they put off the flesh and were joined with Christ in baptism. They had received in Christ both forgiveness and life, and God cancelled the record of debt that stood against them with its legal demands.
- Colossians 2:16-23—Paul warns that they will be disqualified if they put their faith in the false teaching of men. Paul defines the elements of this false teaching.
- Colossians 3:1-17—Paul exhorts them to seek the things that are above where Christ is, for they had died and their lives were hidden with Christ. In Christ, they were being renewed in the knowledge from Christ. Therefore, they are to put to death various sins to avert the wrath of God. They were also to put on certain virtues, and do everything in the name of the Lord Jesus, giving thanks to God the Father through him.
- Colossians 3:18-4:1—Paul delineates rules for Christian households, including those between husbands and wives, between fathers and children, and between masters and slaves. Submission and obedience are commanded of the weaker; love, tenderness, justice and fairness are commanded of the stronger.
- Colossians 4:2-6—Paul exhorts the Colossians to be steadfast in prayer and thanksgiving. He commands them to manifest proper behavior and speech.
- Colossians 4:7-18—Paul gives his final instructions and greetings.

REFLECTIONS

First, Paul exalts Christ with many descriptions. We should also exalt Christ as preeminent because there are some who would diminish Christ in order to insert their own teaching into Christianity. In the context of Colossians, Christ is preeminent over the false teachers who wanted the

Christians to elevate philosophy, empty deceit, human traditions, and the elemental spirits of the world over Christ. We must learn again this lesson, for it appears we have a short memory and these issues reemerge each generation. We must not add to or take away anything from the teachings of Christ and His apostles. Let us not be "disqualified" because we teach as doctrine the commandments of men.

Paul again spends much time defining the Christian life. He again helps us understand by stating it in terms of vices that we must "put to death," and in terms of virtues that we must "put on." We personally must learn these and teach them to brethren. For a Christian there are two ways to live: through virtue which will lead to heaven, or through vice which will lead to hell. These teaching are as ancient as the apostles, and are found repeatedly in manuscripts of the first 500 years of church history.

Therefore, let us restore the exaltation of Christ, and let us restore the Christian life. In so doing, we will be restoring the New Covenant.

1 Thessalonians

The book of 1 Thessalonians was written in about AD 51 to encourage this new church in their faith. Paul especially addresses the eternal state of those Christians who had already died, the second coming of Christ, and godly living.

- 1 Thessalonians 1:1-10—Paul greets the church and expresses thanksgiving. Very notable is Paul's description of their faith, their evangelistic zeal, and their example to all the churches in Macedonia and Achaia. They held Paul as an example and imitated him.
- 1 Thessalonians 2:1 to 3:13—Paul describes his ministry among the Thessalonians and their response. Most notable is Paul's commendation on how they received the word he taught:

> [13] For this reason we also constantly thank God that when you received the word of God which you heard from us, you accepted it not as the word of men, but for what it really is, the word of God, which also performs its work in you who believe. 1 Thessalonians 2:13 (NASB).

Indeed, we must remember that Paul spoke the word of God. Paul speaks of the persecution that all Christians must bear. Paul speaks of his longing for them, his difficulty in returning, and Timothy's encouraging report concerning them.

- 1 Thessalonians 4:1 to 5:22—Paul gives several exhortations. First, he exhorts them to live a Christian life: avoid sexual immorality, show brotherly love, live quietly, mind your own affairs, and to work with your hands. He then teaches them about the second coming of Christ. Paul then gives them several more imperatives regarding Christian living in the church and ends with a benediction.

REFLECTIONS

Oh, may it be so, that all the churches of Christ will be examples in spreading the Word of God. The faith of the Thessalonians was known over a significant part of the region, and that was not long after they had been established as a congregation. Let us imitate the good they did. For those who have planted churches, let us not look at them as a burden, but pray for them and have the same longing for them as did the Apostle Paul. In addition, let us remember that Paul returned to churches he had planted to strengthen them (Acts 14:21-22; 15:41; 16:4-5).

We should continue to study how Paul ministered among the churches. He was intent on helping the churches mature and he did so as a vocational missionary. Under these circumstances, there could never have been an accusation of greed. He was gentle and encouraging. However, he never did it to please man, but only to please God. He never was reluctant to instruct them in the hard issues of living a Christian life. He never engaged in shameful methods such as deception which is commonly practiced today by the "change agents." These "change agents" come into churches saying they believe just as all others in the church, but they do not. As they get into the leadership of the church, they then change practices, such has having musical instruments, expanding women's role into those denied by the New Covenant, diminishing the authority of elders, having the Lord's supper in any kind of meeting on any day, and many other things.

Again, we must restore the authority of the apostles. Their teachings are the word of God. If we don't believe this, then we are not biblical Christians.

We must also seek to be a holy and sanctified people despite the mocking of this by the Western culture.

Defining Christian life and exhorting Christians to live such a life was a major portion of what Paul wrote. It is possible that no other teaching of Paul took up such a lion's share of space in the sacred pages. We must study Paul's inspired understanding of the Christian life closely and teach the virtues of the Christian life to all Christians and warn about the vices.

We must never stop teaching about the Day of the Lord and the consequences of not "watching."

We should understand how we are to function as a church. Paul's 16 imperatives on this should be taught (1 Thessalonians 5:12-22).

In summary, there is much to restore from 1 Thessalonians. However, if we teach and practice these things, we will be restoring the New Covenant in our own generation.

2 Thessalonians

The book of 2 Thessalonians also was written in approximately AD 51. Paul again addresses the second coming of Christ. He also emphasizes again the necessity of working rather than being idle. He had addressed both of these things in his first letter to them, but evidently more questions had been raised so he had to address them again.

- 2 Thessalonians 1:1-12—Paul gives his greeting, thanksgiving, encouragement, and prayer. Paul makes it clear that those who persecute them will be punished by God. He also defines those who will face punishment: those who do not know God and those who do not obey the gospel of our Lord Jesus.

- 2 Thessalonians 2:1-12—Christ's second coming and the man of lawlessness. Paul tells them not to believe anyone who says that Christ had already come again. Rather, Christ's second coming will be strikingly evident to all people. Before Christ comes, the rebellion and the man of lawlessness are revealed. This man of lawlessness will be an atheist, will be against anything relating to any god, and will be the visible head of the church. The mystery of lawlessness was already at work. When the man of lawlessness is revealed, Christ will slay him. The man of lawlessness will be strengthened by Satan with power, false signs, wonders, and wicked deception. Those who do not love the truth and thus do not obey the truth will be condemned. Historically, the following have been suggested as being the man of lawlessness:

1. He was represented by the emperors of Rome, especially Nero and Domitian. Certainly many of the Roman emperors waged campaigns to exterminate all Christians. But this was permanently stopped in A.D. 313 with the edict of toleration by Constantine the Great.
2. He was represented by the Papacy and the hierarchy of the Roman Catholic Church. This was the popular opinion of the protestant reformers. Certainly the Roman Catholic Church became something that did not even remotely resemble the apostolic government of the church in the first century. Many of the Popes were evil and murdered whoever chose to not follow their decrees. The Inquisition by the Catholic Church killed more Christians than all the Roman persecutions of the first three centuries. The Pope that authorized the Inquisition is still considered a saint. Yet, as bad as some of the Popes were, they were not atheists. However, in this time of incredible change, even that may become a reality.
3. The Antichrist will gain dominion briefly before the second coming of Christ and His 1000 year reign on earth (Premillennialists).

4. Not a man, but rather a recurrent spirit or principle of rebellion.
5. It was a speculation by Paul that he borrowed from Babylonian or other ancient mythology. But no evidence for this exists.
6. It is Satan. However, the coming of the man of lawlessness is by the activity of Satan, so the two cannot be the same.

- 2 Thessalonians 2:13-17--Paul gives his second thanksgiving, encouragement, and prayer. Paul says we are called by the gospel. Paul commands them to "…stand firm and hold to the traditions that you were taught by us…."
- 2 Thessalonians 3:1-15—Paul requests their prayers. He then exhorts them and four times mentions "commands" that must be obeyed. Specifically, they are commanded to avoid a brother who is idle. He commands that "If anyone is not willing to work, let him not eat." They were to exclude those who did not follow what Paul wrote in this letter. They were to warn such a person.
- 2 Thessalonians 3:16-18—Paul gives his benediction and his own handwriting on the manuscript as a sign that it was genuine. So there were forgeries circulating that claimed they were written by Paul but were not (2 Thessalonians 2:2).

REFLECTIONS

This is the shortest epistle that was written to a church in the New Testament. However, there are several things here that we must study well and put into practice. First, we must teach the second coming of Christ as something that is still in the future. We must emphasize the global significance of this and especially that God will judge those who do not know Him and those who do not obey the gospel. This should spur us to evangelism. Although America and Europe are now experiencing a hardening of heart toward Christianity, there are many areas of the world that are ripe unto harvest.

We must realize that it is God who makes us worthy. It is also God who will fulfill every resolve for good and every work of faith for His glory.

The man of lawlessness is equivalent to the antichrists who were present during the times of the apostles and are present to this day. Someday this lawlessness will reach a crisis and an atheist will emerge as the great leader. He will have the allegiance of the majority and amaze them with false signs, wonders, and wicked deception. But Christ will destroy him. The second coming of Christ cannot occur until the man of lawlessness is revealed and destroyed. Who is this man of lawlessness of the future? Who can know more than what Paul has written? But we must understand that the man of lawlessness will arise from within the church and be magnified by the visible church; therefore, we must be on guard against all attacks on the Word of God lest we find ourselves drawn into the side of unbelief. Even now, there are many who call themselves Christians but do not believe in the miracle-working, prophecy-fulfilling, dying-an-atoning-death, rising-from-the-dead, and ascending-to-the-Father type of Christ found only in the New Testament. Others have added so much of their own teachings to the teachings of Christ and His apostles that they do not even resemble New Testament Christianity now. They too have become part of that ever-present and symbolic "man of lawlessness."

We are called through the gospel and we must stand firm and hold to the writings of Christ and His apostles. If we turn our backs on these, then we have sown the wind and will reap the whirlwind (Hosea 8:7). Again we must recognize the authority of apostles of Christ and obey their teachings. Apostolic "tradition" is the same as apostolic teachings and doctrines. We must not neglect them.

We must not be idle. We must quietly work for our own food and not expect the church to feed us. We must affirm that if we will not work, then we will not eat.

Surely, there are at least these things that we must obey today. If we do obey and teach these things, we will be restoring the New Covenant.

Study Questions

1. Christ and Paul taught the Two Ways—one way of thinking and living to reach heaven, and the other way of thinking and living to reach hell. Paul clearly taught that Christians should to take the virtues and reject the vices. This was taught by the church for the first five centuries, but then rejected. How can we restore the teachings of the Two Ways today?
2. Gnosticism, or salvation by special knowledge not found in Scripture, was like a plague during the first three centuries of the church. It was reborn when the teachings of men favored cultural values over God's Word. How do we restore the Word of God as being more important than the teachings of men?
3. Paul taught a highly exalted doctrine of Christ, even the absolute preeminence of Christ. Christ and our relationship with Him are the driving forces that enable us to deny sin and live holy and productive lives. How can we restore this highly exalted doctrine of Christ today?
4. Who is the "Man of Lawlessness" who must be made manifest in the visible church before Christ comes again? What precautions must we take?

Chapter 11

New Covenant—1 Timothy to Philemon

The Pauline Epistles as Restoration Documents

1 Timothy

The book of 1 Timothy was written by Paul approximately A.D. 62-64 from somewhere in Macedonia. The purpose of this letter was to direct Timothy in multiple aspects of serving as an evangelist in Ephesus. This was a well-established church with appointed elders (Acts 20:17-38) when Timothy was with them. Paul's theme is as follows:

> [14] I am writing these things to you, hoping to come to you before long; [15] but in case I am delayed, I write so that you will know how one ought to conduct himself in the household of God, which is the church of the living God, the pillar and support of the truth. 1 Timothy 3:14-15 (NASB)

- 1 Timothy 1:1-2—Paul gives Timothy his salutation.
- 1 Timothy 1:3-20—Paul charges Timothy, and first warns about false teachers. These were Jewish in origin, and were teaching inaccurately about the Law. Paul shows the right use of the law in the church, and that is in defining sinful behavior. Paul

emphasizes his own conversion from Judaism to Christianity to show that Christ came into the world to save sinners, of which he was the worst. He magnifies Christ's perfect patience in his own conversion, and blesses the Almighty. He exhorts Timothy regarding the prophecies about him, to wage the good warfare, holding faith and a good conscience. He gives the examples of Hymenaeus and Alexander whose faith had been destroyed and whom Paul had handed over to Satan.

- 1 Timothy 2:1-15—Paul details how prayers should be given in the assembly. Pray for all people because God desires that all be saved and come to the knowledge of the truth. Christ is our only mediator in prayer. Men should lead in public prayer, but women should be silent. The reason for this submission of women in public worship goes back to mankind's fall in the Garden of Eden (Genesis 3:15-16). Her salvation was found in her embracing her traditional roles with faith, love and holiness.
- 1 Timothy 3:1-13—Paul gives the qualifications for overseers. In the first century, overseers (or bishops) and elders referred to the same church office, one term denoting their duty (overseer) and the other their age (elder). These qualifications emphasize character, family, maturity, and their ability to teach. Paul shows the qualifications for deacons and their wives. These emphasize tested character, faith, and family. A detailed comparison of the elder qualifications in Timothy and Titus as well as the deacon and wife qualifications are available upon request.
- 1 Timothy 3:14-16—Paul gives his theme, exalts the church, and proclaims Christ as the mystery of godliness.
- 1 Timothy 4:1-5—Paul prophesies about an apostasy in "later times" when people will devote themselves to demons and their teachings. They will be liars who forbid marriage and require abstinence from foods. A number of current religious bodies would fit these specific properties. Rather, God created food and it should be received with thanksgiving. Our food is made holy by the word of God and prayer.
- 1 Timothy 4:6-16—In this section there are a number of imperatives all directed at Timothy's personal and public life as a preacher of the gospel. If Timothy teaches and practices these

things, he will save both himself and his hearers. Of significant note is Paul's command to Timothy to "devote yourself to the public reading of the Scripture." Sadly, this has fallen into neglect in most churches today.

- 1 Timothy 5:1 to 6:3—In this section Paul instructs Timothy regarding how we should treat the elderly, young men, older women and younger women. He commands that widows be honored by the church, but only if they have no family to support them. If we do not provide for our own family, we are worse than an unbeliever. Qualifications for an enrolled widow are given. An elder who preaches should be considered worthy of double honor (recognition and pay). No accusation against an elder may be considered unless there are two or three witnesses. Unrepentant elders must be publicly rebuked. Timothy is charged not to exercise favor for anyone who sins in this manner. He gives Timothy some medical advice. He gives regulations regarding slaves and masters.
- 1 Timothy 6:3-10—Paul again warns Timothy about false teachers, and gives specific attributes of these people. He gives a strict admonition against the love of money, which is the root of all kinds of evil.
- 1 Timothy 6:11-16—Paul again exhorts Timothy, especially that he "...keep the commandment unstained and free from reproach...." Here Paul speaks of the whole of Christian teachings that we must keep. Paul then extols Christ in the most elevated way.
- 1 Timothy 6:17-19.—Paul gives further instructions to the rich.
- 1 Timothy 6:20-21—Paul give final exhortations to Timothy, "...guard the deposit entrusted to you...." Here again Paul is taking about the whole of Christian teachings and also Timothy's own ministry. So we too are to "keep" and to "guard" what God has given us.

REFLECTIONS

Even though 1 Timothy was written to an evangelist, it was also written to be read by the church in Ephesus, especially the elders and deacons. Paul is intense in this epistle and that means apostasy was probably present in Ephesus and Timothy needed to root it out. As was so common in the Gentile churches, Greek philosophy with myths and false knowledge abounded in the church. This was the "baggage" the Gentiles brought with them when they came to Christ. It was their culture, and it was sometimes difficult for them to see Christianity except through the lens of their pagan culture.

We must learn from the Gentile Christians of that day because we also see Christianity through the lens of our own pagan culture today. We must return to the Bible and understand what it says within its own context. Our job is not to see the Bible through the lens of our own pagan culture, but rather through the lens of the divinely authorized and inspired apostles. Our task is not to make the Bible or the church into something pleasing to our pagan upbringing, but repent and become what is pleasing and obedient to God according to the New Covenant. We must try to see ourselves as God sees us. We must be converted into a biblically holy way of thinking and acting. If we are converted to what man says rather that what God says, we will be condemned.

As an example, consider the children of Israel who were idolaters when God led them out of Egypt. When they turned and obeyed God, they prospered. However, when they returned to their pagan upbringing and worshipped and served idols, they were punished and eventually destroyed as a nation by God. God will surely also judge our cultures today and condemn them because as countries we have turned away from Him to serve materialism and sexual immorality.

Paul preaches Christ's grace in his own conversion and his ministry. Paul preaches the perfect patience of Christ that is available to every man because it was available to him, the worst of sinners. Christ Jesus came into the world to save sinners (1 Timothy 1:15). This is good news. And we should never forget that Christ's primary charge was to save sinners:

> [10] "For the Son of Man has come to seek and to save that which was lost." Luke 19:10 (NASB)

Therefore, we too must make that our top priority. However, we must beware. Many theologians will teach social justice and thinking like Jesus, and these are not bad things to teach. However, when you ask them about saving the lost, they are not sure what to answer as they can't imagine anyone could be really lost. They say that God, if He really does exist, would never send anyone to hell, which they say doesn't exist. They have wandered so far away that the Bible has become irrelevant to them.

Paul has a special concern for the church at Ephesus and gives specific instructions concerning worship and the role of women in the public worship of the church in 1 Timothy 2:8-13. What he taught was countercultural because in the long-standing pagan culture there were female witches, female mediums and priestesses to many of the gods (e.g., 1 Samuel 28:7). However, in the church Paul commands that the women were "...to learn quietly with all submissiveness." We must do all we can to use our Christian sisters in the work of the church for this is very good in the eyes of God and extremely helpful in the work of the church. However, we must never put our Christian sisters into roles that violate the New Testament because this will result in condemnation both for the leaders and for the women involved.

The leadership of the local congregation must be biblical. This means the appointing of qualified men for the works of elders and deacons. The qualifications in 1 Timothy 3 and Titus 1 are numerous. However, they, for the most part, are obtainable. Many of these qualifications are to some extent relative in nature. The issue for potential elders of having a Christian family, and particularly faithful Christian children, is a problem in every culture. However, those who have passed such a test have demonstrated their ability to lead and care for the church. These elders are to "shepherd the flock of God that is among you" (1 Peter 5:2), meaning that each congregation has their own elders who know them and are there to help them.

Paul commands Timothy on many issues related to being an evangelist. The vast majority of these issues need to be implemented by evangelists of our own time. Paul also prophesies a coming apostasy which may have begun in Ephesus at that time. In 1 Timothy 4:1-5 Paul describes the marks of that apostasy and we find that these elements exist today among those who call themselves Christians.

There are so many things we need to understand and restore in order to be the church that Christ wants. We need evangelists who are not afraid to preach the New Covenant. We need elders and deacons who will do what God has called them to do in His Word. This epistle is part of the New Covenant. Understanding it and applying it will cause a restoration of the New Covenant.

2 Timothy

This is the last known epistle that Paul wrote. He was again imprisoned in Rome and awaiting execution. The book of 2 Timothy was written in about A.D. 64-67. In spite of the abandonment of most of his close companions and his own impending death, Paul is steadfast in faith and able to exhort Timothy. He greatly emphasizes Scripture in this epistle as the standard that must prevail when the apostles all died.

- 2 Timothy 1:1-5—Paul gives his greetings to Timothy and his thanksgiving.
- 2 Timothy 1:6-14—Paul exhorts Timothy to endurance in suffering. Timothy must rekindle the gift of God (probably his ministry). Timothy must not be ashamed of Paul's sufferings, but join him in those sufferings. It is God, not man, who saves us and calls us by His grace in Christ, and this purpose was established before the ages began. Christ has abolished death and brought life and immortality to light through the gospel. It is for this that Paul is persecuted. But he trusts in Christ and is not ashamed and has full confidence. He commands Timothy to

  [13] Retain the standard of sound words which you have heard from me, in the faith and love which are in Christ Jesus. [14] Guard, through the Holy Spirit who dwells in us, the treasure which has been entrusted to you. 2 Timothy 1:13-14 (NASB) (See also Psalm 19:7-11; Matthew 5:18; 1 Corinthians 2:10-

13; 4:17; 2 Timothy 3:16-17; 2 Peter 1:20-21; 2 Peter 3:15-16.)

- 2 Timothy 1:15-18—Paul contrasts the unfaithful (Phygelus and Hermogenes) with the faithful household of Onesiphorus who attended to Paul in prison and was not ashamed of his chains. Paul prays for mercy on Onesiphorus in the Day of the Lord.
- 2 Timothy 2:1-13—Paul commands Timothy to be strengthened by Christ's grace. Paul again charges Timothy that this pattern of sound words (2 Timothy 1:13) that Timothy has heard him speak he must entrust to faithful men who can teach others also (2 Timothy 2:2). Paul then gives brief illustrations of commitment, including a soldier, an athlete, and a farmer. He must remember Christ and endure persecution. Timothy must remember Paul in his chains and endure persecution. The goal is salvation, for if we die with Christ, we live with Christ; if we endure with Christ, we will reign with Christ. However, if we deny Him, He will deny us. If we become faithless, that does not change the faithfulness of Christ.
- 2 Timothy 2:14-26—Paul continues to exhort Timothy in multiple aspects. Paul warns Timothy of an apostasy from two false teachers, Hymenaeus and Philetus, who taught that the resurrection had already happened. Paul also warns Timothy about controversies and tells him to avoid such. Paul contrasts virtues and vices to illustrate what Timothy must do and teach. In the midst of conflict, Timothy should be patient and correct gently.
- 2 Timothy 3:1-9—Paul warns Timothy of the sinfulness of the "last days" and tells him to avoid people who manifest these sins.
- 2 Timothy 3:10-17—Since Timothy had followed every aspect of Paul's ministry, Paul warned Timothy again about suffering and persecution with the implication that Timothy will have to endure the same. He admonishes Timothy to continue in what he has learned from Scripture, and holds up Timothy's mother and grandmother as his teachers in this regard from his childhood. Such Scriptures can make Timothy wise for salvation through faith in Christ. Obviously this refers to the Old Testament Scriptures. Indeed, the entire gospel can be preached from Isaiah

alone. Because of his own impending death, Paul shows Timothy the confidence Timothy can have in the Scripture by making this phenomenal statement:

> [16] All Scripture is inspired by God and profitable for teaching, for reproof, for correction, for training in righteousness; [17] so that the man of God may be adequate, equipped for every good work. 2 Timothy 3:16-17 (NASB)

- 2 Timothy 4:1-5—Paul continues his exhortation to Timothy by commanding him to preach, be ready always, reprove, rebuke and exhort with patience and teaching. Paul foretells that there will come a time when people will not endure sound teaching.
- 2 Timothy 4:6-9—Paul says he is ready for death, he has done all he could, and he will receive a reward from the Lord. He hastens to say that all who have loved Christ's appearing will also received such a reward.
- 2 Timothy 4:9-18—Paul gives Timothy multiple personal instructions regarding co-workers, regarding coming to him with certain items and bringing Mark, regarding enemies, regarding Luke only being with him, regarding his first defense and how the Lord was with him, and regarding his confidence of a safe deliverance to Christ's heavenly kingdom.
- 2 Timothy 4:19-22—Paul gives his final greetings.

REFLECTIONS

Paul once again pours out his heart to Timothy, and this reflects the close relationship between the apostle and Timothy. Paul emphasizes Scripture throughout this epistle knowing that as he and the other apostles died, the Christians would have to rely on the Scriptures as being their source of authority in religion. Paul had a strong message for Timothy regarding his duties as an evangelist and his responsibility to remain faithful even when persecuted. Paul even called on Timothy to share in those sufferings. Paul's visions of the last days reveal a horror beyond words. But they were there in Paul's time, and they are here in our time also. Someday the man of lawlessness will be revealed fully. In fact, there are many "preachers" who are presently working for denominations who don't believe in the Bible and deny the evidence that Christ presented in John 5:30-47. They keep their jobs by preaching what they do not believe. Therefore, we may not be so far away from the "man of lawlessness" as we might think.

The evangelist today must understand what Paul says to Timothy and obey it. We all must understand the authority of Scripture, hear it, and do it. If we start trusting God's word rather than that of men, then we will be on our way to restoring the New Covenant in our own time.

Titus

Paul wrote the book of *Titus* in approximately AD 63. Like 1 Timothy, Titus was written after Paul's first Roman imprisonment, and there are many similarities between these two epistles. Moss says that only Titus 2:11-14 and 3:3-7 have no corresponding content in 1 Timothy (Moss, 1994, p. 134). Paul and Titus went to Crete and planted several churches. Paul then left Crete, but Titus stayed behind to help mature the churches there. Paul wrote this brief epistle to assist Titus in his ministry there. This epistle was not just for Titus, however, since Paul addresses the church in the final sentence.

Crete is a large island in the Mediterranean Sea and had long been associated with mainland Greek language and culture. Crete was conquered by the Romans in 69 BC. The indigenous culture were known as "liars, evil beasts and lazy gluttons" (Titus 1:12). To say a person was like a Cretan was to say they "played the liar" (Unger, 1957, 1961, 1966, 1985, pp. 226-227). Jews also lived on the island of Crete (Acts 2:11). However, there is evidence they were involved in Jewish myths (Titus 1:14) and also wanted to bring Jewish practices such as circumcision into the church (Titus 1:10).

- Titus 1:1-4—Paul greets Titus.
- Titus 1:5-16—Paul gives instructions to Titus regarding appointing elders in every town on the island of Crete. Paul first gives the qualifications for "elders," and uses the word "overseer" or

"bishop" interchangeably with the word "elder." This shows that these two terms were synonymous in the first century. Detailed analysis of the qualifications of elders and deacons are available upon request. In addition, Paul shows what the elders' must be able to rebuke the false teachers. In the process Paul reveals the unsavory reputation of the Cretans.

- Titus 2:1-15—Paul commands Titus to teach sound doctrine, and then directs what Titus should teach to older men, older women (who should also teach younger women), younger men, and slaves. God's grace and salvation teaches us to renounce evil and embrace virtues and good works. He repeatedly refers to God and His salvation for us in Christ.
- Titus 3:1-11—Paul continues with multiple exhortations regarding the Christian life. They must respect their government and all people. The Cretan Christians must live in this manner because God sent Christ to save them. He gives final instructions on dealing with false teachers who will not repent.
- Titus 3:12-15—Paul sends his final instructions and greetings.

REFLECTIONS

There were multiple problems in the newly formed churches on the island of Crete. The Jewish factions were causing their usual problems, and the indigenous people had their own cultural baggage. Patient and firm teaching of "sound doctrine" by Titus and others would be the only means to reeducate the new converts so that they could serve God in spirit and in truth. This "sound doctrine" consisted of the gospel as well as stipulations about how one must live the Christian life. Specifically, this included both what the Christian must do and what the Christian must not do. If we have limited our "sound doctrine" to the five things necessary for salvation and the five acts of worship, then we must learn to think like Paul. Paul is very concerned about what we believe about Christ and how we live the Christian life. We must be engaged in good works. Many times we in the churches of Christ have been legalistic about the 5/5 principles mentioned above, but have been poor in good works. The early Christians organized themselves to spread the gospel, take care of orphans and minister to the sick and the poor. We should not surrender those things we have found true in the Bible about salvation and worship. However, we must do a better job with the Christian life, especially good works.

God's chosen way of church government was and still is by way of the elders, and this was honored by the apostle Paul since the time of his first missionary journey (Acts 14:23). Paul gives extensive qualifications for the selection of elders. These are high standards compared to their cultural norms. However, the only effective tool available for the evangelist in this matter is the word of God and patient teaching with encouragement. Changes can and will come if prospective elders and deacons will commit these things to prayer, and if they will lead their families in a loving and faithful service to God.

Truly, if we are doing what Paul commanded Titus, we will be restoring the New Covenant.

Philemon

- Philemon 1-3—Paul greets Philemon.
- Philemon 4-7—Paul describes Philemon's love, faith, and service to Christians; Paul prays for Philemon.
- Philemon 8-22—Paul pleads that Philemon would forgive Onesimus and receive him as a brother in Christ. Paul hopes that Philemon will allow Onesimus to help Paul in the ministry. Paul promises to pay any expense incurred by Onesimus' actions. Paul hopes to visit Philemon soon.
- Philemon 23-25—Paul gives his final greetings.

REFLECTIONS

Paul wrote to Philemon of Colosse, the owner of the slave Onesimus in approximately AD 60. Onesimus had run away from Philemon and probably had stolen some things from Philemon. Onesimus found Paul in the Roman prison and Paul converted him to Christ. Paul pleads with Philemon to show mercy toward Onesimus, and to treat him "...no longer as a slave but more than a slave, as a beloved brother...." Paul offered to pay Philemon for any loss he may have suffered in regard to Onesimus' running away. Paul wanted Philemon to free Onesimus so Onesimus could serve Paul in the gospel. In a society where one-third of the people were slaves rather than Roman citizens, Paul communicated a message of social justice, grace, and mercy to Philemon. This was a bold letter from one Christian to another, and at its very base was the system of Roman slavery versus Christian brotherhood (1 Corinthians 12:13). Later Church History in about AD 300 indicated that Philemon did free Onesimus, and that this specific Onesimus became a bishop in Borea of Macedonia (Anonymous, Constitutions of the Holy Apostles, Book VII, Chapter XLVI, 1997). We should note that Paul did not take a stand as a radical social reformer regarding slavery. Had he made his emphasis slavery rather than Christ, then the spread of Christianity in the Roman Empire would have failed. However, that did not keep him from having these kinds of private communications as we read about in Philemon. Elsewhere, Paul admonished slaves to obey their earthly masters as if serving Christ (Ephesians 6:5-8; Colossians 3:22-25; 1 Timothy 6:1-2; Titus 2:9-10; see also 1 Peter 2:18). However, Paul also encouraged them to "gain their freedom" if they had such an opportunity (1 Corinthians 7:21). Therefore, this short letter written by Paul to Philemon was of considerable significance to any Christian who owned slaves.

Even today, this epistle strongly challenges us to love our neighbor as we love ourselves, and never regard a brother of humble means as inferior to ourselves. If we do these things, then we will be about God's business of restoring the New Covenant in our own time.

Study Questions

1. What should we do if we find a false teacher among us?
2. Paul made sure there were elders in all the churches he planted. Must we use the qualifications Paul wrote in 1 Timothy 3 and Titus 1, or are we free to make up our own qualifications?
3. Paul charged Timothy to "devote yourself to the public reading of the Scripture." However, it is clear that we don't read the Scriptures publicly as they did in the 1 and 2 centuries. If Timothy was devoted to this, how often would he have done this? In what

ways can we increase the public reading of the Scriptures?

4. Paul commanded Timothy to "keep the commandment," "guard the deposit," and "hold fast the sound pattern of words." How can we be sure we are reading, teaching and holding fast to the whole counsel of God today?
5. How can we be sure we are viewing the Scriptures through the lens of Christ and His apostles rather than through the lens of culture?
6. Using Titus 2:1 to 3:11, define "sound doctrine."
7. What does the short letter to Philemon teach us today?

Chapter 12

New Covenant—Paul's Points

Prominent Points in the Pauline Epistles

This is a summary of the prominent points found in the Pauline Epistles. This is not an exhaustive list. The purpose is to show not all of his doctrines, but rather what Paul appears to comment on the most.

Regarding God and Christ

1. God is the Righteous Judge of every person (Romans 1:18-3:20).
2. We will be accursed by God if we add to or take away from the gospel (Galatians 1:6-10).
3. God did not spare His Son, but gave Him up for us all (Romans 8:32).
4. Christ came into the world to save sinners (1 Timothy 1:15 and see Matthew 9:13; Luke 19:10).
5. God delivered us from the domain of darkness and transferred us to the kingdom of His beloved Son, in whom we have redemption, the forgiveness of sins (Colossians 1:13-14).

6. God foreknew, predestined, called, justified, and glorified Christians to be conformed to image of Christ and be sealed with the Holy Spirit (Romans 8:28-30; Ephesians 1:3-14).
7. If God is for us, who can be against us? Nothing can separate us from the love of God (Romans 8:31-39).
8. God's sovereign choice was to choose the remnant of the Jews as well as Gentiles for salvation (Romans 9:1 to 10:21; 15:8-13).
9. God commissioned Paul to be a minister to the Gentiles (Romans 15:14-21).
10. Christ is the power of God and the wisdom of God (1 Corinthians 1:24).
11. Christ is our wisdom, righteousness, sanctification and redemption (1 Corinthians 1:30).
12. The foolishness of God is wiser than men, and the weakness of God is stronger than men (1 Corinthians 1:25).
13. God chooses the foolish and the weak to overcome all things against the Gospel (1 Corinthians 1:26-29).
14. God is the God of all comfort (2 Corinthians 1:3-4).

Regarding the Church

1. God's plan for the church goes back ages before Christ was born (Ephesians 3:9).
2. It is through the church that the manifold wisdom of God is revealed (Ephesians 3:10).
3. Christ loved the church and gave Himself up for her (Ephesians 5:25).
4. Christ sanctifies and cleanses the church by the washing of water with the word that the church may be holy and without blemish (Ephesians 5:26-27).
5. Christ nourishes and cherishes the church (Ephesians 5:29).
6. Christ is the head of the church, which is His body, the fullness of Him who fills all in all (Ephesians 1:22-23; 4:15; 5:23; Colossians 1:18; 2:10, 19).
7. Warnings about divisions in the church (1 Corinthians 1:10-17; 3:1-22; 11:18).

8. Paul taught every church the fundamentals of Christianity (1 Corinthians 4:17).
9. The church is to leave the judgment of outsiders to God (1 Corinthians 5:12).
10. The church must judge those inside the church (1 Corinthians 5:12; 6:4).
11. The four-fold leadership of the church (Ephesians 4:11).
12. The tasks this four-fold leadership must accomplish (Ephesians 4:12-16).
13. We must do everything so that the church can be edified (1 Corinthians 14:4-5, 12).
14. Paul wrote his first epistle to Timothy so that we may know how we ought to behave in the household of God, which is the church of the living God, a pillar and buttress of the truth (1 Timothy 3:15).
15. Paul provides prerequisites to having unity in the church (Ephesians 4:1-3).
16. Paul provides 7 things, without which true unity in the church is impossible (Ephesians 4:4-6).

Regarding God's Righteousness, Salvation, & Justification

1. This is the theme of Romans (Romans 1:16-17).
2. The righteousness of God through faith in Jesus Christ for all those who believe (Romans 3:21-26; Galatians 2:15-21; Ephesians 2:1-10; Philippians 3:7-10; see John 4:10; 1 Peter 1:5).
3. Abraham and David were justified by faith rather than by works (Romans 4:1-25).
4. Consequences of being justified by faith—peace, access by faith into His grace, joy, hope, endurance, eternal life, with God's love in our hearts (Romans 5:1-21).

God Graciously Grants us a Responsive Faith

1. (To hear the gospel with understanding is a gift from God: Luke 24:45; John 3:27; 6:44, 65; Acts 16:14.)

2. Godly grief (i.e., the knowledge that we have hurt God/Christ with our sins) leads to repentance. God graciously grants us that privilege to repent (Romans 2:4; 2 Corinthians 7:10; 2 Timothy 2:25).
3. We can only make the good confession that Jesus Christ is Lord through the enabling of the Holy Spirit (1 Corinthians 12:3); this confession of faith is necessary for salvation (Romans 10:9-10; see also Matthew 10:32-33, Mark 8:38; Luke 12:8-9; 1 John 2:23; 4:15).
4. God unites us with Christ's death, burial and resurrection in baptism. It is the baptism that God ordained. We consider ourselves dead to sin and alive to God in Christ Jesus. We become slaves to righteousness. The free gift of God is eternal life in Christ Jesus our Lord (Romans 6:1-23; 1 Corinthians 12:13; Galatians 3:27).
5. In baptism, God washes us, sanctifies us, and justifies us in the name of the Lord Jesus Christ and by the Spirit of our God. This is God's washing of regeneration (1 Corinthians 6:11; Ephesians 5:26; Titus 3:5).
6. Rather than the Mosaic Law, the law of the Spirit of life in Christ Jesus sets us free from the law of sin and death. There is no condemnation for those who are in Christ Jesus (Romans 8:1-11).

Regarding Life in the Spirit

1. The Spirit of Christ dwells within Christians (Romans 8:9-11).
2. We are heirs with Christ (Romans 8:12-17).
3. We have the hope of future glory, and we wait patiently for it (Romans 8:18-25).
4. The Spirit intercedes for us in prayer (Romans 8:26-27).
5. For those who love God, all things work together for good (Romans 8:28).

Regarding Jews and Gentiles

1. Jews and Gentiles are both judged guilty by God (Romans 1:18 to 3:20).

2. Both can be saved only through Christ (Romans 3:21-30).
3. The Jews failed because they pursued a law of works for righteousness. They failed because it was not by faith but by works. However, the Gentiles pursued righteousness by faith and succeeded (Romans 9:1 to 11:36).

Regarding the Mosaic Law

1. Even the Jews are released from the Mosaic Law, including the 10 commandments, and must die to the Law (Romans 7:1-8; Galatians 2:15 to 3:14; Philippians 3:2-11).
2. God set us free from the Mosaic Law, and it is fulfilled by loving our neighbor as ourselves (Galatians 5:13-15).
3. The Mosaic Law exposes and makes known our sins, but has not power to save us from that sin. As result, we become increasingly sinful and miserable in our guilt. (Romans 7:7-25).
4. Christ is the end of the law for righteousness to everyone who believes (Romans 10:4-13).
5. The role of the Mosaic Law in Christianity (Galatians 3:15 to 4:31).
6. The role of circumcision in Christianity (Galatians 5:1-12; 6:11-16).
7. The Mosaic Law is fulfilled by loving our neighbors as ourselves (Galatians 5:13-15; 6:2 and see Matthew 7:12; 22:37-40).

Regarding Support for Preachers

1. Support from the local church (Romans 10:14-15; 1 Corinthians 9:7-14; Galatians 6:6).
2. The model of Paul, the self-supported vocational (tent-making) preacher (Acts 18:3; 20:34; 1 Corinthians 4:12; 9:12, 15; 2 Corinthians 11:7; 1 Thessalonians 2:9; 2 Thessalonians 3:8).
3. Occasional missionary support for Paul from a church that Paul started (Philippians 4:10-19).

Regarding the Christian Life

1. We are to be living sacrifices to God, not conformed to this world, but transformed by the renewing of our minds (Romans 12:1-2).
2. God gives to the members differing gifts according to His wisdom (Romans 12:3-8).
3. The Two Ways (virtues we must have and vices we must avoid) (Romans 12:9 to 15:7; 16:17-20; Galatians 5:16 to 6:10; Philippians 1:27 to 2:18; 3:12 to 4:9; 1 Thessalonians 4:1 to 5:28; 2 Thessalonians 2:13 to 3:15; Titus 2:1 to 3:11).

Regarding Preachers

They must read 1 & 2 Timothy and Titus carefully and understand all the commands so they might follow them. Non-preachers will also benefit greatly from these books as well.

Regarding Examples of What Should be Taught and Preached

1. Preach Christ who was crucified, buried, resurrected, appeared to many people, ascended to God the Father, and now is the one and only head of the church (1 Corinthians 1:23; 2:1-5; 15:1-11; Colossians 1:15-23).
2. Preach about the second coming of Christ (1 Thessalonians 4:13 to 5:11; 2 Thessalonians 1:5-10).
3. Teach about the Man of Lawlessness who must come before Christ's return (2 Thessalonians 2:1-12; 1 Timothy 4:1-4; 2 Timothy 3:1-9).
4. Teach what the gospel is:

    - It is the death, burial and resurrection of Christ (1 Corinthians 15:1-4; 2 Timothy 2:8).
    - It is the appearances of Christ to the 500, James, the apostles, and Paul (1 Corinthians 15:5-8).
    - The gospel includes all the contents of the four Gospels

(Mark 1:1).

- It is the final judgement (Romans 2:16).
- The gospel must be obeyed (Romans 10:16).
- If we don't obey the gospel, we face the wrath of God (2 Thessalonians 1:8).
- The gospel must be confessed (2 Corinthians 9:13).
- We must not receive another "gospel" (2 Corinthians 11:4; Galatians 1:6-9).
- Never allow any additions or subtractions from the all-sufficiency of the gospel of Christ which saves us (Galatians 1:6-10).
- Our conduct must be in step with the gospel (Galatians 2:14).
- Our conduct must be worthy of the gospel (Philippians 1:27).
- The gospel gives us hope (Colossians 1:23).
- The gospel is the key to unlock blessings for all nations (Galatians 3:8).
- The gospel is the good news of our salvation (Ephesians 1:13).

5. God will judge all people (Romans 1:18 to 3:20).
6. God's justification of us is by His grace through our faith in Christ and not by meritorious works of the Mosaic Law (Romans 1:16-17; 4:1 to 5:21; Galatians 2:15 to 4:31).
7. Preach against divisions in the church (1 Corinthians 3:1-23).
8. Teach the ministry of the apostles (1 Corinthians 4:1-20).
9. Avoid sexual immorality (1 Corinthians 5:1-13; 6:12-20).
10. We must disfellowship church members who are sexually immoral, greedy, idolaters, revilers, drunkards or swindlers if they refuse to repent (1 Corinthians 5:1-13).
11. Don't have lawsuits against believers (1 Corinthians 6:1-8).
12. The unrighteous will not inherit the kingdom of God—therefore, repent (1 Corinthians 6:9-11).
13. God's principles for marriage (1 Corinthians 7:1-39).
14. Warning against idolatry (1 Corinthians 8:1-13; 10:1-33).
15. The surrendering of our "rights" in order to further the gospel (Romans 15:1-7; 1 Corinthians 9:1-27).
16. The role of women in the church (Romans 16:1-16; 1 Corinthians

11:1-16; 14:33-40; 1 Timothy 2:8-15; 3:11; 5:3-16; Titus 2:3-5; see also Acts 18:26).

17. Teach the Lord's Supper (1 Corinthians 11:17-34).
18. Teach the history of miraculous spiritual gifts (1 Corinthians 12:1-31; 14:1-40; see also Acts 8:14-17).
19. Teach the superior gifts of faith, hope, and love, and the superiority of love (1 Corinthians 13:1-13).
20. Teach the resurrection of the dead and the resurrection body (1 Corinthians 15:12-58).
21.
22. Teach the principles for the weekly contribution (1 Corinthians 16:1-4; 2 Corinthians 8:1 to 9:15).
23. Teach the basic principles for churches sharing in benevolence (2 Corinthians 8:16-24).
24. We also must join the apostles in their ministry of reconciliation (2 Corinthians 5:11-21).
25. It is possible to fall from grace and to be severed from Christ. This was due to adding to the gospel the need for circumcision to save us. We must never add to or take away from the gospel (Galatians 5:4).
26. Teach Christ's humility as our example of humility (Philippians 2:1-11).
27. We should imitate Paul (1 Corinthians 4:16; Philippians 3:17; 4:9; 2 Thessalonians 3:7-9).
28. We should stand firm and hold to the teachings of Paul (1 Corinthians 11:2; 2 Thessalonians 2:15; 3:6; 2 Timothy 1:13; 2:2).
29. We should allow no other doctrine to come into the church (1 Timothy 1:3-11).
30. We should have the biblical pattern of local church leadership only, which is elders and deacons (Philippians 1:1; 1 Timothy 3:1-13; Titus 1:5-16 and see also Acts 14:23).
31. We must preach the word even if people don't want to hear it (2 Timothy 4:1-5).
32. Teach sound doctrine (Titus 2:1-15).
33. Teach the implications of Philemon—for example, the beginning of the end of slavery or the way we must love our neighbor as ourselves, even if that person is poor or uneducated, etc.

Regarding Inspiration

1. Divine wisdom from the Holy Spirit was given to the Apostles (1 Corinthians 2:6-16).
2. God appointed the apostles to be ministers of the New Covenant and ministers of reconciliation (2 Corinthians 3:1 to 7:1).
3. The inspiration and all-sufficiency of Scripture (2 Timothy 3:16-17 and see also Romans 15:4; 2 Timothy 1:13; 2:2; 2 Peter 1:20-21).
4. Paul's teachings are the Word of God, not the word of men (1 Thessalonians 2:13 and see also Galatians 4:14 and Matthew 10:20).

Regarding Paul's Apostleship

1. Paul's defense of his apostleship (2 Corinthians 10:1-18; 12:11-21; Galatians 1:1).
2. Paul versus the false apostles (2 Corinthians 11:1-15).
3. Paul's sufferings as an apostle (2 Corinthians 11:16-33).
4. Paul's vision and his thorn in the flesh (2 Corinthians 12:1-10).
5. Paul's severe warning to the Corinthians (2 Corinthians 13:1-10).
6. Paul received gospel directly by revelation from Christ and not from any other person (Galatians 1:11-24).
7. Paul and his gospel were accepted by the other apostles (Galatians 2:1-10).
8. Paul rebuked Peter because he was not in step with the truth of the gospel (Galatians 2:11-14)

Study Questions

1. What does Paul say about God and Christ?
2. What does Paul say about the church?
3. Describe God's role (rather than man's role) in our salvation:

What does God do for us regarding hearing, repentance, the good confession, and baptism?

4. Describe the relationship Christians should have with the Mosaic Law today.
5. What are the three means of preacher support in the New Testament? What are the advantages and disadvantages of each?
6. What are Paul's views on inspiration?
7. Defend Paul as being a real apostle. What are your evidences?

Chapter 13

God's Covenant of Marriage

God's View of Marriage

God introduced the concept of marriage in the Garden of Eden making marriage the second oldest covenant in recorded history. Although it is not called a "covenant" or "marriage" there, God formed Eve from Adam's rib as a helper fit for him. Because woman was taken out of man, Adam said she was "bone of my bones and flesh of my flesh" and thus named her "Woman." God was the witness to this relationship. Therefore, God proclaimed the conditions of that marriage covenant:

> [24] For this reason a man shall leave his father and his mother, and be joined to his wife; and they shall become one flesh. Genesis 2:24 (NASB)

That marriage is a covenant before God and God is the witness to it is explicitly stated in Malachi:

> [13] And this second thing you do. You cover the LORD's altar with tears, with weeping and groaning because he no longer regards the offering or accepts it with favor from your hand. [14] But you say, "Why does he not?" Because the LORD was witness

> between you and the wife of your youth, to whom you have been faithless, though she is your companion and your wife by covenant. [15] Did he not make them one, with a portion of the Spirit in their union? And what was the one God seeking? Godly offspring. So guard yourselves in your spirit, and let none of you be faithless to the wife of your youth. [16] "For the man who hates and divorces, says the LORD, the God of Israel, covers his garment with violence, says the LORD of hosts. So guard yourselves in your spirit, and do not be faithless." Malachi 2:13-16 (ESV)

It is also implied in Proverbs 2:17 that marriage is a covenant between the husband and wife and God is the witness of that covenant.

God chose to use the language of marriage to describe His own covenant relationship with Israel. When both Israel and Judah turned away from Him, the word God brought through the prophets was that He was the husband of the descendents of Jacob (Isaiah 54:5; Jeremiah 3:14, 20; 31:31-32; Ezekiel 16:8, 15-16, 32; Hosea 2:16). God's disappointments, pain, anguish and anger at the spiritual adultery of His people is spelled out graphically in Hosea's relationship with Gomer, the prostitute, who became his unfaithful wife. The pain of Hosea in Gomer bearing illegitimate children even while she was his wife was symbolic of the anguish God had for His unfaithful and idolatrous people Israel for whom He was the rightful husband (Hosea 2:7-9).

Through the prophets God also chose the language of divorce to communicate that since His people, Israel, broke covenant with Him, He would also annul the blessings of His covenant for them (Isaiah 50:1; Jeremiah 3:8). Yet, God took Judah back when they returned from 70 years of Babylonian captivity (Hosea 2:16, 19-20).

When Christ came, He also used the language of marriage to symbolize His relationship with the church. His bride was not the children of Israel, but the church (2 Corinthians 11:2; Ephesians 5:22-33). The symbolic fulfillment of that relationship will be in heaven (Revelation 19:6-9; 21:2).

Therefore, there is abundant evidence from Scripture that marriage is a covenant between a husband and wife in which God also shares His Spirit in that union. God is therefore an ever-present and irremovable part of the marriage covenant. God also is a witness to the marriage covenant and will bring judgment on those who break it.

However, in the Western Culture as well some other cultures, the institution of marriage is under attack. It is wounded and is actually in danger of dying. Although the AIDS epidemic has somewhat blunted the tsunami of free love with multitudes of sex partners in both the straight and gay communities, sexual immorality is still thriving like a foul and frothing cesspool. Sexual intercourse without commitment and certainly without marriage is continuously portrayed in TV, movies and novels as normal and healthy. Living in fornication before marriage is now the assumed norm. Virginity until marriage is despised among many of the youth. To our great shame, this civilization is decaying rapidly and is running away from the God of the Bible as fast as it can. God has never tolerated this kind of thing—it has always marked the ending of a culture and the certainty of divine vengeance. In the midst of this intense and increasing fornication, 1 Corinthians 7:1-40 still stands as a witness to God's plan for men and women from the beginning of time. This was God's will from the beginning:

> [18] Then the LORD God said, "It is not good for the man to be
> alone; I will make him a helper suitable for him." [19] Out of the
> ground the LORD God formed every beast of the field and every
> bird of the sky, and brought them to the man to see what he would
> call them; and whatever the man called a living creature, that was
> its name. [20] The man gave names to all the cattle, and to the birds
> of the sky, and to every beast of the field, but for Adam there was
> not found a helper suitable for him. [21] So the LORD God caused
> a deep sleep to fall upon the man, and he slept; then He took one
> of his ribs and closed up the flesh at that place. [22] The LORD God
> fashioned into a woman the rib which He had taken from the man,
> and brought her to the man. [23] The man said,
> "This is now bone of my bones,
> And flesh of my flesh;
> She shall be called Woman,
> Because she was taken out of Man."
> [24] For this reason a man shall leave his father and his mother, and

> be joined to his wife; and they shall become one flesh. [25] And the man and his wife were both naked and were not ashamed. Genesis 2:18-25 (NASB)

Therefore, from the beginning of time it was, and still is the will of God that there be one man with one woman for life. The man and woman are to "leave parents," "be joined" and "become one flesh." Perversions of God's plan came later with Lamech who decided to have two wives (Genesis 4:19, 23), and his example caused many others to have multiple wives (Genesis 6:2-3). Because of this God brought the flood on the earth to destroy all people except for Noah and his family. Please note that Adam had only one wife despite the fact that he lived 930 years (Genesis 5:5). Noah was the man God selected to preserve the human race, and he also had only one wife despite the fact he lived 950 years (Genesis 9:29). Even still later the practice of homosexuality in Sodom was punished by God and the first case of incest is described with Lot and his daughters (Genesis 19). The offspring of this incest were Moab (the father of the Moabites) and Ben-ammi (father of the Ammonites). Both these nations were continual enemies of God's chosen people, the Israelites. Therefore, man has been in constant rebellion against God from the dawn of our existence regarding God's plan for marriage.

When God made His Covenant with Israel through Moses, God knew that their hearts were so hard that they, like their forefathers, would not adhere to His pattern of one man with one woman for life (Matthew 19:7-8). Therefore God permitted divorce in the Mosaic Covenant because of their hard hearts, yet even that had its limits:

> [1] "When a man takes a wife and marries her, and it happens that she finds no favor in his eyes because he has found some indecency in her, and he writes her a certificate of divorce and puts it in her hand and sends her out from his house, [2] and she leaves his house and goes and becomes another man's wife, [3] and if the latter husband turns against her and writes her a certificate of divorce and puts it in her hand and sends her out of his house, or if the latter husband dies who took her to be his wife, [4] then her former husband who sent her away is not allowed to take her again to be his wife, since

> she has been defiled; for that is an abomination before the LORD, and you shall not bring sin on the land which the LORD your God gives you as an inheritance. Deuteronomy 24:1-4 (NASB)

Christ's Teaching on Marriage

However, when Christ came as the Son of God, our Savior, the Messiah, the Lord Jesus Christ, He was straight-forward about God's demands regarding marriage-divorce-remarriage in the New Covenant (Matthew 5:31-32; 19:3-9; Mark 10:11-12; Luke 16:18; Romans 7:3; 1 Corinthians 7:10-11). Christ took the issue not back to Moses, but all the way back to the Garden of Eden where there was to be one man with one woman for life. Jesus took the issue back before there were ever any Jews or Gentiles. He took it back to the parents of all people everywhere:

> [3] Some Pharisees came to Jesus, testing Him and asking, "Is it lawful for a man to divorce his wife for any reason at all?" [4] And He answered and said, "Have you not read that He who created them from the beginning MADE THEM MALE AND FEMALE, [5] and said, 'FOR THIS REASON A MAN SHALL LEAVE HIS FATHER AND MOTHER AND BE JOINED TO HIS WIFE, AND THE TWO SHALL BECOME ONE FLESH'? [6] So they are no longer two, but one flesh. What therefore God has joined together, let no man separate." [7] They said to Him, "Why then did Moses command to GIVE HER A CERTIFICATE OF DIVORCE AND SEND her AWAY?" [8] He said to them, "Because of your hardness of heart Moses permitted you to divorce your wives; but from the beginning it has not been this way. [9] And I say to you, whoever divorces his wife, except for immorality, and marries another woman commits adultery." Matthew 19:3-9 (NASB)

As we can see, Jesus quotes what God said from the very beginning, but adds what was logically present in the Garden of Eden in verse 6: "What therefore God has joined together, let no man separate." Therefore, the only divorce God will approve of in the New Covenant is in the case of "sexual immorality." In this case, the innocent partner can divorce and remarry, but the guilty partner cannot remarry.

We must understand this word "immorality" or "sexual immorality." This Greek word in Matthew 19:9 is πορνεία and it means fornication, sexual immorality and sexual sin in a general sense that includes many behaviors (Swanson, 1997), or "every kind of unlawful sexual intercourse" (Bauer, Arndt, Gingrich, & Danker, 1979, p. 693). Thayer defines it as "illicit sexual intercourse" and this includes adultery, fornication, homosexuality, lesbianism, intercourse with animals, sexual intercourse with close relatives, and sexual intercourse with a divorced man or woman (Thayer, 1999). In essence, any sexual intercourse outside of a biblically legal marriage between a husband and wife is πορνεία. This means that premarital sex is also πορνεία.

Since there can be no doubt about what Jesus said, many who call themselves Christians today strive to find some loophole in Christ's teachings that they might be allowed to divorce and remarry as they wish rather than as Christ commanded. The following are some objections to Christ's Law being applied today:

1. Some say that Christ's command was only for the Jews and is not binding on the Gentiles. However, Christ went back to the Garden of Eden before there was ever a Jew or a Gentile, showing that His teaching applied to all people. In addition, John the Baptist rebuked Herod Antipas (the tetrarch) for having Herodias as his wife (she was his niece) because she had been his brother Philip's wife prior to Herod wooing her away into adultery (Matthew 14:3-4; Leviticus 18:16; 20:21). Therefore, John the Baptist made marriage in the Mosaic Law apply to the Idumaean (that is, from Edom) Herod Antipas. Now the entire Herodian Family Tree was Idumaean, and Herod Antipas had not one drop of Jewish blood in his veins (Dosker, 1939, 1956). Yet in spite of these things, John the Baptist used the Mosaic Law to rebuke Herod. If the Mosaic Law regarding these matters applied to an Edomite in John's time, does not Christ's Law regarding marriage, divorce and remarriage apply to us today who call ourselves Christians?
2. Some say that what Jesus spoke in the Gospels is not applicable for us today since the New Covenant didn't start with Matthew 1:1 but with Acts 2. They thereby nullify Christ's command to

the apostles in Matthew 28:20—"...teaching them to observe all that I have commanded you." Here the word that is translated "observe" is τηρέω and it means "to continue to obey orders or commandments" (Louw, 1996, c1989). Therefore, we are obligated to teach and obey exactly what Christ commanded.

3. Others would say that the resurrected and ascended Lord Jesus Christ gave to Paul something that would supersede what Christ has previously commanded. They claim that Christ revealed more permission to Paul in 1 Corinthians 7 and that we need to go by that additional revelation rather than by Matthew 19:9. This is called by the scholars the "Pauline privilege" and they allege that Paul makes an allowance in 1 Corinthians 7:15 of divorce and remarriage when the unbelieving spouse leaves (DeMoss, 2001).

James O. Baird has carefully studied eight different positions on divorce and remarriage and describes them in detail. A summary of these eight positions are as follows:

1. Death is the only cause for remarriage.
2. Divorce and remarriage are approved for the innocent party in the case of fornication.
3. Divorce and remarriage are approved if these happened before baptism because the sin was washed away.
4. Divorce and remarriage are approved if these happened before baptism because they were not subject to Christ's Law.
5. Believer forsaken by unbeliever is free to remarry.
6. Both parties in the divorce are free to remarry if the cause is fornication.
7. Divorce and remarriage are approved for any legal cause.
8. Divorce and remarriage are approved as this requires no cause at all (Baird, 1981, pp. 18-22)

Is There A Pauline Privilege in 1 Corinthians 7?

Now it should be obvious that there cannot be 8 or 15 or 100 different explanations of marriage-divorce-remarriage in the eyes of God. There can be only one. Matthew 19:9 is clearly depicted in choice number 2. Does the "Pauline privilege" really exist in 1 Corinthians 7? This is why I researched and wrote a commentary on 1 Corinthians 7. However, including the entire treatment of 1 Corinthians 7 is not practical in this book that is focused on God's Covenants and Restorations. Therefore, I will summarize the salient points and leave the reader to decide based on the evidence.

Paul did not command marriage except for the one who could not exercise self-control and burned with passion. Celibacy was encouraged because of the then-present Jewish persecution of Christians. Further, Paul, being a prophet, undoubtedly foresaw the fierce and brutal Roman persecutions starting in about a decade after the time of his writing First Corinthians. At that time Nero would torture and brutally murder countless thousands of Christians for his own entertainment in Rome. Again, this was the reason Paul recommended celibacy so frequently in this chapter.

Because of the risk of sexual immorality, Paul recommended that each man and woman have a mate. The husband and the wife are treated equally, especially regarding sexual obligations. In Paul's discussion of this, it is apparent that he speaks directly to marriages in which both the husband and wife are Christians. He says of this kind of marriage,

> [10] But to the married I give instructions, not I, but the Lord, that the wife should not leave her husband [11] (but if she does leave, she must remain unmarried, or else be reconciled to her husband), and that the husband should not divorce his wife. 1 Corinthians 7:10-11 (NASB)

Here the words "leave" and "divorce" are from two different Greek words. However, both these Greek words were used in the first century to describe divorce. BDAG (Bauer, Arndt, Gingrich, & Danker, 1979, p. 890) indicates that χωρίζω (chōrizō) clearly speaks of divorce in 1 Corinthians 7:11, 15a, and 15b. Louw and Nida agree, and they make this observation regarding the usage of ἀφίημι and χωρίζω:

> Some persons have attempted to make an important distinction between ἀφίημι in 1 Cor 7.11, 13 and χωρίζω in 1 Cor 7.15 on

> the assumption that ἀφίημι implies legal divorce, while χωρίζω only relates to separation. Such a distinction, however, seems to be quite artificial. (Louw, 1996, c1989)

Therefore, Paul's description of marriage between Christians in First Corinthians 7:10-11 leaves no room for divorce. However, if there is a divorce, then the man and the woman have no option except remaining unmarried or being reconciled. There is no possibility for remarriage to a different person for either spouse after a divorce between two Christians. In this Paul appears to be more conservative than what Jesus commanded in Matthew 19:9. Paul's understanding of God's will on this issue is the same as is found in Mark 10:11-12 and Luke 16:18.

Paul then addresses marriage between a Christian and a non-Christian in 1 Corinthians 7:12-16. The Christian spouse is commanded not to divorce. However, if the unbelieving spouse does divorce the Christian spouse (translated "separates" in many English versions despite the known meaning as related by Louw above), then the Christian "is not enslaved." Many people today say this means the Christian can remarry according to Paul. However, the Greek word translated "enslaved" is never used to describe marriage in the Bible. Rather, the word translated "enslaved" in 1 Corinthians 7:15 means to be under obligation (Swanson, 1997). It means that one person gains control over another so that they will serve their own interests (Louw, 1996, c1989). It expresses the total binding of another person (Friedrich, Pitkin, Kittel, & Bromiley, 1964-c1976).

When the unbelieving partner separates (i.e., divorces), the believing partner must not allow that person to enslave them or to make them subservient to the unbeliever's interests. In other words, the unbelieving partner has no rights to come back and have sex or participate in any other privileges that a functional marriage relationship would imply. Holladay phrases it in this manner: "Here the meaning is that the believing spouse is not obligated to make what are obviously futile attempts to maintain the relationship" (Holladay, 1984).

This much seems plain from the text. However, some people infer great liberties from this text which are highly questionable interpretations of the Greek text. For instance, some would say that Paul made "separation" a valid cause for divorce, thus adding "separation" to "sexual immorality," which was Christ's only justification for divorce and remarriage as stated in Matthew 19:9. However, this inference is based on a misunderstanding of the Greek word, which means divorce, not separation. Therefore, Paul did not authorize divorce because of separation because he was not talking about "separation" but divorce in the Greek text.

Another example of an inference of great liberty is the misinterpretation of "not enslaved." Although this clearly means that the unbeliever who has divorced the believer has no right to enslave the believer to do his or her will after divorcing, these writers say that this term means that the believer is free to remarry. However, the Greek text does not say anything about remarriage here. Paul clearly addresses remarriage in 7:39, but he does not do so in this verse.

In my opinion, there are serious problems with the proposal that Paul has created a new right for a divorced believer to remarry in 7:15. These are as follows:

1. Paul did not say anything about remarriage in 7:15. Any attempt to make him say something about remarriage is groundless inference.
2. It is evident in 1 Corinthians 7:14 that God recognizes the marriages of believers to unbelievers, and is willing to work with those marriages, even to the point of granting ritual sanctification to the unbelieving spouses and the children of such marriages. Since God is so committed to these marriages, it would be surprising to find He has a different standard for the believing mate in this setting than He expressed regarding believer/believer couples in 7:10.
3. As part of the summary statement to the entire chapter, in 7:39a we have read the following:

   1 Corinthians 7:39 (ESV) [39] A wife is bound to her husband as long as he lives.

   Whereas the first expression of this thought in 7:10 is in the context of marriage between believers, this last occurrence has no such limitations, and appears to be a summary thought for the whole chapter that addresses all marriages involving Christians. In 7:10 if the believing wife separates (i.e., divorces) her husband, she should either "remain unmarried or else be reconciled to her husband." That is, she is divorced by civil law, but is still viewed as having a husband by God. So in 7:39 this principle is reinforced, and without limitations concerning which kind of marriage it applies to. Therefore, Paul's summary statement in 7:39 does not support that he has created a new reason for divorce and remarriage.

4. Instituting such a rule for remarriage in 7:15 would impose a duel standard upon the church. Believer-believer marriage would have one standard (no remarriage), but believer-unbeliever marriage would have another (can remarry). It is obvious that any believer who understood this would tend toward marrying an unbeliever, because if it didn't work out, the believer could remarry. Such a double standard in the early church would have been very confusing and divisive as well as unsupportive of the believer-believer marriage.
5. Although Jesus said that the Holy Spirit would guide the apostles into all truth (John 16:13), he also commanded the apostles to teach all believers to observe "all that I have commanded you" (Matthew 28:20). If it is true that Paul intended to introduce these freedoms in 1 Corinthians 7, surely he would have been more exact in his words and even mentioned "remarriage" in 7:15 as he did in 7:39 and as Christ did in Matthew 19:9. The absence of such a clear reference to "remarriage" in 7:15 brings great doubt on the contention that Paul introduced another justification for remarriage in 7:15.
6. There is no evidence from early church history that they understood Paul to have given another justification for a Christian to be divorced and then remarried. Rather, we find the following comment by Caverno:

That neither Paul nor anyone else ever put such construction upon his language, is evidenced by the fact that there is no record in history of a single case where it was attempted for 400 years after Paul was in his grave, and the Roman Empire had for a century

> been Christian. Then we wait 400 years more before we find the suggestion repeated. That no use was ever made of such construction of Paul in the whole era of the adjustment of Christianity with heathenism is good evidence that it was never there to begin with. So we shall pass Paul as having in no respect modified the doctrine of divorce laid down by Christ in Mt 19. (Caverno, 1956)

The last major issue regarding the marriage-divorce-remarriage controversy has to do with Paul's rule in all the churches, namely, that

> [20] Each man must remain in that condition in which he was called. 1 Corinthians 7:20 (NASB)

Specifically, Paul applies this rule to the Christian/unbeliever marriage, circumcision, and slavery. The point is that none of these three issues keep one from becoming a Christian. Circumcision has no religious significance in Christianity. Being a slave is not a sin, although Paul encouraged Christian slaves to seek their freedom if possible. Likewise, being married to an unbelieving spouse does not prevent one from becoming a Christian. Paul's entire discussion of this rule is meant to buttress his command that the Christian should not divorce his/her unbelieving spouse. To apply this rule to some sinful condition, for example, such as lying, stealing, or fornication, is not at all what Paul was writing about. Rather, such sinners must repent of such sins and not "remain in that condition in which he was called." Therefore, this rule must be used only within the context that Paul clearly established in this chapter.

The only time Paul actually addresses the "remarriage" issue is in First Corinthians 7:39, which says,

> [39] A wife is bound as long as her husband lives; but if her husband is dead, she is free to be married to whom she wishes, only in the Lord. 1 Corinthians 7:39 (NASB)

Therefore, we see the same permanence in marriage as Paul gave in 1 Corinthians 7:10-11. But Paul adds here, "only in the Lord," to indicate the Christian widow or widower can only marry a Christian.

Summary of Paul's Points in 1 Corinthians 7

The purpose of this careful look into 1 Corinthians 7 was to discover particularly what Paul taught about marriage, divorce, and remarriage. With that in mind, I will summarize the points Paul made. However, I need to emphasize that I am addressing here only what Paul taught in 1 Corinthians 7:1-40, and not what Jesus taught about marriage, divorce and remarriage in Matthew 19:9.

1. Paul favors marriage in order to prevent sexual immorality, and he says the husband and wife must address the other's sexual needs. The only exception to this obligation is a mutual decision to forgo sex for a limited time in order to devote themselves to prayer (1 Corinthians 7:2-5).
2. Marriage is not commanded of anyone, except those who cannot exercise self-control (1 Corinthians 7:2, 9).
3. Marriage is not a sin for the unmarried, virgins, and widows (1 Corinthians 7:8, 28, 36).
4. Celibacy is consistently encouraged for all who are considering marriage, and who can practice celibacy without sinning (1 Corinthians 7:6-9, 25-35, 37, 40).
5. Marriage is a permanent yoking together by God, and this bond, in God's sight, can be broken honorably only by a partner's death (1 Corinthians 7:10-11, 39). Only in this circumstance of the death of a mate does Paul say the Christian widow or widower can remarry, but "only in the Lord" (1 Corinthians 7:39).
6. SPECIFIC ISSUES CONCERNING MARRIAGE BETWEEN CHRISTIANS:
    a. Divorce is not allowed in a marriage between Christians (1 Corinthians 7:10-11).
    b. If a partner in a marriage between Christians does divorce, then that partner must remain unmarried or be reconciled to their mate (1 Corinthians 7:10-11).
7. SPECIFIC ISSUES CONCERNING MARRIAGE BETWEEN A BELIEVER AND AN UNBELIEVER:
    a. Paul commands the believer to NOT divorce the unbeliever

if the unbeliever consents to stay with the believer (1 Corinthians 7:12-13).

b. God grants ritual sanctification to the unbeliever and the children of this marriage (1 Corinthians 7:14).
c. If the unbeliever divorces the believer, then the believer should accept this and be at peace (1 Corinthians 7:15).
d. If the unbeliever divorces, then the believer is "not enslaved." This means that the believer is not to allow the unbeliever to coerce him/her into any sort of enslavement or control after this divorce (1 Corinthians 7:15).
e. Paul wants the believer to try to convert the unbelieving spouse (1 Corinthians 7:16).
f. Paul exhorts the believer to remain in the marriage with the unbeliever by giving his rule: "remain in the condition in which he is called." He illustrates this with issues of circumcision/uncircumcision and slavery/freedom (1 Corinthians 7:17-24).
g. We must not view marriage as more important than our faith in Christ and our commitment to Christ (1 Corinthians 7:29-35).

Conclusion

In conclusion, the alleged "Pauline privilege" and every other kind of trickery to keep Matthew 19:9 from being the law on Christian marriage are nothing but myths. If anything, Paul's presentation in 1 Corinthians 7 is more conservative than Matthew 19:9. Church history confirms that no one in the first 800 years of Christianity took Paul's statement in 1 Corinthians 7:15 as a justification for remarriage. Rather, the church fathers looked with suspicion on any second marriage, even when a marriage was broken by death of a spouse. For them, the dissolution of a marriage by divorce or death was an opportunity for greater devotion and service to God as a single person. And if one considers the amount of space Paul gives to celibacy in this chapter, I would suggest that the church fathers had a better grasp of 1 Corinthians 7 than we do in America today.

Study Questions

1. When and where did God establish the Covenant of Marriage?
2. Is God a witness to every marriage?
3. Is marriage called a "covenant" in Malachi 2:13-16?
4. Does God make the husband and wife one, with a portion of the Spirit in their union?
5. Describe Hosea's marriage with Gomer and how God was symbolically a husband to the Jews.
6. Who is the bride of Christ now?
7. According to Matthew 19:9, what is the only reason God will recognize for a legal divorce?
8. What does "sexual immorality" mean?
9. In 1 Corinthians 7:10-11, does Paul allow divorce between a husband and a wife who are both Christians?
10. In 1 Corinthians 7:12-17, does Paul want a marriage between a believer and a non-believer to end in divorce?
11. If the non-believer divorces the believer, does Paul say clearly that the believer can remarry?
12. What does the word "enslaved" mean in 1 Corinthians 7:15?
13. What does "remain in the condition in which he was called" (1 Corinthians 7:20) mean? What three things did Paul apply this rule to? Can we apply it today to any sinful condition? For example, is a person to remain a liar or a thief when they become a Christian since they are to "remain in the condition in which he was called"?
14. Describe what the only acceptable reason is for remarriage in 1 Corinthians 7:39.
15. Was Paul given any special privileges regarding marriage/divorce/remarriage that were not previously granted by Christ in Matthew 19:9?

Conclusions

Conclusions Regarding God's Covenants and Restorations

Covenant with Adam

Chapters 1 through 5 show the covenants God made in the Old Testament and the restorations of those covenants. We found that Adam and Eve failed in their faith and obedience to God. They believed a "change agent" named Satan who, just like the change agents of today, lied to both Adam and Eve to get them to change their faith from God to Satan. Satan is the father of lies and deception. All those who use lies and deception belong to Satan. Adam and Eve died that day spiritually, and then died a physical death later. Death spread to all people because all sinned. What Satan said would not happen did happen. Our only hope is in the seed of the woman who would come and conquer Satan—Christ Jesus, our Lord and Savior.

Covenants with Noah and Abraham

Both Noah and Abraham were giants of faith. Both of them had long-term relationships with God. It didn't matter what God commanded, they obeyed it without murmuring or complaining. Many of the things God commanded them were huge and their daily obedience to these things lasted for more years than we live today. The faithful Noah by his obedience gave humans the chance to survive a deeply wicked generation. Being saved by water is a foundational concept for Christian baptism. The faithful Abraham became the prototype of real faith, and it characterizes the very faith we as Christians must have. Abraham's faith and God's justification of Abraham by that faith became the foundational concept of our justification by God's grace through faith in Christ. The very way we are saved under the New Covenant is immersed heavily in the symbolism of God's Covenants with Noah and Abraham. God seems very pleased to restore elements of those covenants for us today.

Covenant with Israel through Moses

The next covenant we studied was the Mosaic Covenant. We are not under the Mosaic Covenant today. However, our knowledge of it is essential to our understanding the New Covenant. For instance, we are not under the 10 commandments today. Nevertheless, all the expectations of those commandments, with the exception of keeping the Sabbath, were brought forward into Christianity. The sundry laws regarding human conduct are foundational for the very laws we live under today. Many of the basic regulations we have in the New Testament are based on commandments in the Mosaic Covenant. However, we do not have any of the Levitical laws concerning animal sacrifices. Yet, we must understand that these Levitical laws were a type of what Christ's sacrifice on the cross would become. Just as an innocent lamb had to die bearing the sins of a Jew under the Mosaic Covenant, so also the Lamb of God also had to die bearing all our sins in His body on the tree in the New Covenant. Just as the blood from an innocent lamb was poured on the horns and on the sides of the altar for the forgiveness of sins before the Almighty in the Mosaic Covenant, so also the blood of the Lamb of God had to be shed for the forgiveness of our sins in the New Covenant and presented before the Almighty in heaven (Hebrews 9:11-14).

In addition, the Mosaic Covenant is an astounding document from a scientific standpoint. None of the harmful cures from ancient Egypt can be found in the Mosaic Covenant. Rather, we find rules of sanitation and isolation that were thousands of years ahead of when man would rediscover them. How did Moses know that circumcision on the eighth day was the safest time to perform this surgery on a newborn? What Moses commanded regarding circumcision in 1446 BC was not understood scientifically until the 1900's. How could Moses be 3300 years ahead of his time in terms of scientific knowledge? Therefore, the Mosaic Covenant shows an incredibly advanced wisdom that could only have come from God. So the Mosaic Covenant was indeed inspired, and the commandments contained therein are holy.

The evidences concerning the restorations of God's Covenant with Moses are even more astounding. Moses himself restored that Covenant by reading it again to the Israelites and commanding that it be read every seven years. More restorations of the Mosaic Covenant were accomplished by Joshua, the Judges, the good Judean kings and priests, the prophets, Jeshua, Zerubbabel, Ezra, Nehemiah, and the Persian Kings Cyrus and Artaxerxes. The Maccabees also restored the Mosaic Covenant during those 400 years of prophetic silence before the coming of Christ.

However, the Mosaic Covenant was nailed to the cross with our Savior. It was part of what Christ was referring to on the cross when He said, "It is finished." One major reason the Mosaic Covenant had to retire is that it could only inform the worshippers of their sins. It had no power to rescue the worshippers from their sins. The key to real repentance, life change, and peace with God comes only with the knowledge of who Christ is, what He has accomplished for us, and what our relationship with Him means.

Covenant with Jesus

Most of this book examines the New Covenant. The New Covenant was prophesied by the prophets in the Old Testament. Christ is that New Covenant. Therefore, the concept of covenant is radically changed when we consider the New Covenant. The core of the Gospel became the death, burial, and resurrection of Christ. The Gospels are foundational and are the cornerstones of our faith. They present prophecies concerning Christ, His life, His miracles, His teachings, His sufferings, His vicarious death on the cross, and His resurrection from the dead. Jesus Himself defined the legal defense concerning Himself being the Son of God. One cannot become a biblical Christian unless he/she believes these facts of the Gospels.

The book of Acts is the Christian's book of early church history, showing the spread of Christianity from Jerusalem to Judea, Samaria, and to the uttermost parts of the known earth. In Acts we find the accounts of numerous conversions, and see that the apostles of Christ were very faithful to Christ's great commission just as they were faithful in everything they practiced and preached. The church was first formed in Jerusalem, and the rest of the New Testament is all about Christ and His church. We also see that there was no central agency for the churches on earth, and no visible head of the churches on earth either. Rather, we find individual self-ruling congregations which cooperated with other self-ruling churches. Christ is the only head of the church. We learned that the government of each church was through their own elders. We also learned about the autonomy of the individual churches regarding issues of opinion. However, they had no autonomy regarding issues of doctrine, but answered directly to Christ.

Next we reviewed the Pauline epistles. We found that Paul spent most of his time writing about and extolling God and Christ, and instructing us about the Christian life by continuously putting before us the Two Ways. There were certain heresies that Paul had to rebuke because, if followed, these would result in damnation of the Christians. We discovered that Paul's epistles were counter-cultural just as Christ's teachings were counter-cultural. Because men wished the church to follow their teachings rather than the teachings of Paul, Paul's epistles were increasingly suppressed beginning in the second century. They were rediscovered by the reformers, and also rediscovered by the founders of the American Restoration Movement. Unfortunately, the Roman Catholic Church and the vast majority of the denominations of today also suppress the Pauline epistles. The liberal theologians attack these epistles in order to destroy their authority. They want to "free" Christianity from Paul's commandments regarding the church. They do this so that Christians will instead follow the religions that the liberal theologians love to create.

Covenant of Marriage

The last covenant we studied was God's Covenant of marriage. Regarding marriage, this has been a sore point with God even from our earliest history. It is clear what God wanted in the Garden of Eden and thereafter. He had to compromise His own values on this subject just to work with the hard-headed and stiff-necked sons of Israel. Jesus Christ restored what God wanted regarding marriage by referring back to God's foundation of marriage in the Garden of Eden. Only Matthew records the exception Christ spoke in Matthew 19:9. We demonstrated from 1 Corinthians 7 that Paul did not have a special "Pauline Privilege" from the Lord. Yet, man is still hard-hearted and slow to comprehend the mind of God. God wants marriage to be permanent: one man and one woman for as long as they live. Let the husband be true the wife of his youth, and let wife be true to the husband of her youth. The only honorable way to end a marriage is if God does it with the death of a spouse. Everything else is like trying to see through muddy water.

What Should be Restored?

One might reasonably ask, "What, then, must we restore?" This is a timely and very appropriate question. Clearly we must restore the teachings of the New Testament. We must live that life. We must follow those commands. By studying the prior covenants, we gain a great understanding regarding what needs to be restored in the New Covenant. For instance, in considering the restorations of the Mosaic Covenant, we must restore the worship that God commands in the New Covenant. However, this cannot be just a restoration in form. It must also be a restoration of the heart, soul, mind, and strength regarding worship. The prophets of the Old Testament decried worship that was superficial and didn't come from the heart. They also condemned worship that did not correspond to a holy lifestyle.

On the basis of his review on this subject of restoration, Ken Kesse has suggested that the following areas should be restored:

1. What we must preach
2. What should be believed and done in order to be saved
3. The pattern of the New Testament church
   a. Worship
   b. Organizational structure
   c. Works and practices
   d. The Christian's lifestyle (Kesse, January 2011)

I believe that Brother Kesse has made some very important suggestions.

I would also suggest that we must look closely to the commands, examples, and necessary inferences throughout the New Testament. These standards of interpretation honor the biblical text. We cannot just "feel" our way through the New Testament. We must greatly desire to understand what God wants us to do, and then do it with all our might. If we do not follow His commands, then we do not know or love God. Consider the following Scriptures:

> [15] "If you love Me, you will keep My commandments." John 14:15 (NASB)

> [21] "He who has My commandments and keeps them is the one who loves Me; and he who loves Me will be loved by My Father, and I will love him and will disclose Myself to him." John 14:21 (NASB)

> [23] Jesus answered and said to him, "If anyone loves Me, he will keep My word; and My Father will love him, and We will come to him and make Our abode with him." John 14:23 (NASB)

> [10] "If you keep My commandments, you will abide in My love; just as I have kept My Father's commandments and abide in His love." John 15:10 (NASB)

> [3] By this we know that we have come to know Him, if we keep His commandments. 1 John 2:3 (NASB)

> [3] For this is the love of God, that we keep His commandments; and His commandments are not burdensome. 1 John 5:3 (NASB)

> [6] And this is love, that we walk according to His commandments. This is the commandment, just as you have heard from the beginning, that you should walk in it. 2 John 1:6 (NASB)

For the Christian, the New Testament documents are all restoration documents. These New Testament documents restore the ancient order of Christianity. There is no other order of Christianity that is approved by God. Therefore, we must restore the New Covenant by restoring the apostolic writings. Just as the Mosaic Covenant was restored by so many people over 1500 years, so we as New Testament Christians must also take our stand and restore the New Covenant for the church today. We must turn away from the teachings of men that have encrusted and massively deformed the New Covenant over the past 2000 years. We must go back to the Bible. We must repent for laying our Bibles aside and not reading and obeying the New Covenant. We must repent for following the teachings of men instead of following God's New Covenant in Christ. Our churches must become devoted to the public reading of Scriptures. We must again become the people of the Book. We must understand the mind of our covenant-making God from the Garden of Eden until now. We must become convinced that we too must obey God's New Covenant.

If we choose the teachings of men instead of the teachings of Christ and His apostles, God says our religion is vain:

> [6] And He said to them, "Rightly did Isaiah prophesy of you hypocrites, as it is written:
> 'THIS PEOPLE HONORS ME WITH THEIR LIPS,
> BUT THEIR HEART IS FAR AWAY FROM ME.
> [7] 'BUT IN VAIN DO THEY WORSHIP ME,
> TEACHING AS DOCTRINES THE PRECEPTS OF MEN.'
> [8] "Neglecting the commandment of God, you hold to the tradition of men." Mark 7:6-8 (NASB)

This means God will not accept our religion if we elevate the teachings of men over the teachings of Christ and His apostles. All our going to church will do nothing for us in His sight. It is like going to school every day and getting a zero every day. Such a record will certainly not be of any use for us, but rather would become a crippling burden for us.

However, if we are truly trying to obey Him, then this will show our genuine faith to God, and He will show us His continuing grace, mercy, and love. Indeed, we will be restoring the New Covenant if we do these things.

Bibliography

Anonymous. (1997). Constitutions of the Holy Apostles, Book VII, Chapter XLVI. In A. Roberts, J. Donaldson, & A. C. Coxe (Eds.), The Ante-Nicene Fathers Vol VII: Translations of the writings of the Fathers down to AD 325 (p. 478). Oak Harbor: Logos Research Systems.

Anonymous. (2010). The Autonomy of the Local Church. Retrieved December 30, 2010, from In Search of the Truth: http://www.insearchoftruth.org/articles/autonomy.html

Baird, J. O. (1981). And I Say Unto You... Nashville: 21st Century Christian.

Bauer, W., Arndt, W. F., Gingrich, F. W., & Danker, F. W. (1979). A Greek-English Lexicon of the New Testament and Other Early Christian Literature. Chicago, London: The University of of Chicago Press.

Bruce, F. (1943, 1946, 1950, 1960, 1981). The New Testament Documents: Are They Reliable? Grand Rapids and Cambridge, MI, USA and UK: WB Eerdmans Publishing Co.

Caverno, C. (1956). Divorce. In J. Orr (Ed.), The International Standard Bible Encyclopaedia (Vol. II, p. 866). Grand Rapids: Wm B Eerdmans Publishing Co.

Clemens, T. F. (1997). Fragments of Clemens Alexandrinus, Chapter III. In A. Roberts, J. Donaldson, & A. C. Coxe (Eds.), The Ante-Nicene Fathers Vol. II: Translations of the writings of the Fathers down to AD 325. Oak Harbor: Logos Research Systems.

DeMoss, M. S. (2001). Pocket Dictionary for the Study of New Testament Greek (electronic ed.). Downers Grove: InterVarsity Press.

Dosker, H. E. (1939, 1956). Herod. In J. Orr, J. L. Nuelsen, E. Y. Mullins, M. O. Evans, & M. G. Kyle (Eds.), The International Standard Bible Encyclopaedia (Vol. III, pp. 1381-1382). Grand Rapids: Wm B Eerdmans Publishing Co.

Dosker, H. E. (1939, 1956). Nazarene. In J. Orr, J. L. Nuelsen, E. Y. Mullins, E. O. Morris, & M. G. Kyle (Eds.), The International Standard Bible Encyclopaedia (Vol. III, p. 2123). Grand Rapids: Wm B Eerdmans Publishing Co.

Ferguson, E. (1996). The Church of Christ: A Biblical Ecclesiology for Today. Grand Rapids, MI/Cambridge, U.K.: William B Eerdmans Publishing Co.

Friedrich, G., Pitkin, R., Kittel, G., & Bromiley, G. W. (Eds.). (1964-c1976). Theological dictionary of the New Testament (electronic ed ed.). Grand Rapids: Eerdmans.

Hailey, H. (1993). A Commentary on the Minor Prophets. Religious Supply, Inc.

Holladay, C. R. (1984). The First Letter of Paul to the Corinthians: Living Word Commentary (electronic ed ed.). Abilene: ACU Press.

The Apostolic Fathers: Greek Texts and English Translations (Vol. third). (1992, 1999, 2007). (M. H. Holmes, Trans.) Grand Rapids, MI: Baker Academic.

Irenaeus. (1997). Irenaeus Aganst Heresies, Book III, Chapter XV. In A. Roberts, J. Donaldson, & A. C. Coxe (Eds.), The Ante-Nicene Fathers, Vol I: Translations of the writings of the Fathers down to AD 325. Oak Harbor: Logos Research Systems.

Josephus, F. Antiquities of the Jews (Vol. 11).

Kesse, K. (January 2011). See that you build according to the pattern shown you Heb 8:5. In B. C. Elders (Ed.), Behold the pattern: 2nd Annual Restoration Workshop (p. 43). Kumasi: Bomso Church of Christ.

Kirby, P. (2001-2011). Martyrdom of Polycarp. Retrieved May 8, 2011, from Early Christian Writings: http://www.earlychristianwritings.com/martyrdompolycarp.html

Lipscomb, D. (1896). A Commentary on the Acts of the Apostles. Nashville: Gospel Advocate Company.

Louw, J. &. (1996, c1989). Greek-English Lexicon of the New Testament: Based on Semantic Domains. (Electronic edition). New York: United Bible Societies.

Lusk, D. T. (1994). God of the Covenant: A Study of Biblical Covenants. David T Lusk.

Moss, C. M. (1994). The College Press NIV Commentary: 1, 2 Timothy & Titus. Joplin: College Press Publishing Co.

Pamphilus, E. (1997). The Church History of Eusebius. In P. Schaff (Ed.), The Nicene and Post-Nicene Fathers Second Series, Vol I. Oak Harbor: Logos Research Systems.

Reese, G. L. (1976, 2002). New Testament History: A Critical and Exegetical Commentary on the Book of Acts. Moberly: Scripture Exposition Books.

Robinson, G. L. (1939, 1956). Solomon. In J. Orr, J. L. Nuelsen, E. Y. Mullins, M. O. Evans, & M. G. Kyle (Eds.), The International Standard Bible Encyclopaedia (Vol. IV, p. 2823). Grand Rapids: Wm B Eerdmans Publishing Co.

Rogers, R. (2002). Life of Christ: A Survey of the Life and Teachings of Jesus. Lubbock: Sunset Institute Press.

Stewart, T. (2001). Apologetics 2: New Discoveries That Confirm the Bible. Lubbock, TX: Sunset International Bible Institute.

Swanson, J. (1997). Dictionary of Biblical Languages with Semantic Domanis: Greek (New Testament). (electronic). Oak Harbor: Logos Research Systems, Inc.

Thayer, J. (1999). Thayer's Greek Definitions (electronic ed.). El Cajon: Institution for Creation Research.

Unger, M. F. (1957, 1961, 1966, 1985). Unger's Bible Dictionary. Chicago: Moody Press.

Vadney, V. J. (2010). Becoming A Mature Christian: Fundamental Principles and Necessary Leadership, Volume 1. Abilene: Desert Willow Publishing.

CPSIA information can be obtained at www.ICGtesting.com
Printed in the USA
LVOW041756061011

249372LV00002B/5/P

9 780983 032724